D1524364

Medieval Times

BY
FRANK EDGAR, Ph.D.
AND GEORGE LEE

ISBN 1-58037-055-1

Printing No. CD-1830

Mark Twain Media, Inc., Publishers
Distributed by Carson-Dellosa Publishing Company, Inc.

INTRODUCTION

Voltaire wrote: "History never repeats itself, man always does." As much as we in the time approaching the year 2000 would argue that the people of the Middle Ages were far different from ourselves, we see some troubling similarities: plagues and diseases without cures, those looking for quick riches in unlikely places, poverty created by war, gangs of barbarians frightening the peaceful, people ready to justify any action by claiming it is done for a "noble purpose," arguments over church and state, and wide gaps between the haves and have-nots.

This brief look spans a period of more than 1,000 years, from about 325 A.D. to 1453 A.D. and beyond. Life changed during that time, and those who lived in 1300 had a much better life than those living in 600. Still, life was hard by our standards, and luxuries were few. For the student who is beginning to discover the past, the authors hope this book will be of some help. Like other books, it is only a small step toward truly understanding how people lived in a time and culture distant from our own.

—THE AUTHORS

TIME LINE

A time line helps us understand the order in which events occurred. We use time lines all our lives. We say that we were born in ____ and started school in _____; we moved to our new home in _____," etc. In the same way, time lines help us keep historical events in sequence. This time line will help you keep events of the Middle Ages in order.

324-337	Constantine emperor of Rome.
325	Council of Nicaea.
330	Constantinople is constructed.
5th century	Angles, Saxons, and Jutes invade England.
406	Vandals invade Gaul (France).
410	Visigoths plunder Rome.
429	Vandals move into Africa.
431	Franks begin moving into Gaul.
452	Attila invades Italy.
476	Fall of Rome.
568	Lombards invade Italy.
570-632	Life of Mohammed.
587	Visigoths in Spain become Catholic.
711-19	Moslems conquer Spain.
714-41	Charles Martel "mayor of the palace" in France.
732	Battle of Tours.
800	Charlemagne crowned emperor by the Pope.
871-899	Alfred the Great is king of England.
987-996	Hugh Capet is king of France.
1066	William the Conqueror leads Norman invasion of England.
1073	Gregory VII named as Pope.
1077	Henry IV (Holy Roman Emperor) does penance at Canossa.
1095	First Crusade.
1147-49	Second Crusade.
1170	Murder of Thomas à Becket in England.
1189-99	Richard I is king of England.
1189-92	Third Crusade.
1192-94	Richard I of England is held hostage.
1202-04	Fourth Crusade.
1212	Children's Crusade.
1215	King John signs Magna Carta in England.
1217-21	Fifth Crusade.
1226-70	Louis IX is king of France.
1228-29	Sixth Crusade.
1245-54	Seventh Crusade.
1265	Simon de Montfort's Parliament in England.
1278	Eighth Crusade.
1294-1303	Boniface VIII is Pope.
1295	Model Parliament in England.

1296	*Clericos Laicos.*
1302	*Unam Sanctum.*
1309-77	"Babylonian Captivity" of the church.
1337	Beginning of Hundred Years' War between England and France.
1346	English victory over French at Crécy.
1356	King John of France captured at Battle of Poitiers.
1358	Jacquerie Rebellion in France.
1381	Wat Tyler Revolt in England.
1382	Wycliffe's followers publish Bible in English.
1413-22	Henry V is king of England.
1415	English defeat French in Battle of Agincourt.
1415	John Huss executed by Council of Constance.
1417	Council of Constance ends Great Schism in church.
1429	Charles VII crowned French king.
1431	Death of Joan of Arc.
1453	English lose all territory in France except Calais.
1453	Constantinople falls to the Muslims.
1455-85	War of the Roses in England.
1461-83	Reign of Louis XI in France.
1469	Marriage of Ferdinand and Isabella unites Aragon and Castile in Spain.
1485	Henry VII becomes English king and establishes the House of Tudor.
1492	Columbus reaches the New World.
1498	Vasco da Gama reaches India.

Roman numerals are used throughout the book to identify kings and Popes. In the Middle Ages, Arabic numbers like we use were not known. The key numbers in the Roman system were **I** (1), **V** (5), **X** (10), **L** (50), **C** (100), **D** (500), and **M** (1000).

Here is a list of Roman numerals that will help demonstrate how the system works:

I (1)	II (2)	III (3)	IV (4)	V (5)	VI (6)
VII (7)	VIII (8)	IX (9)	X (10)	XI (11)	XII (12)
XIII (13)	XIV (14)	XV (15)	XX (20)	XL (40)	L (50)
LX (60)	XC (90)	C (100)	CI (101)	CD (400)	D (500)
DX (510)	CM (900)	M (1000)	MI (1001)	MX (1010)	MCDLII (1452)

Charles VII was the seventh ruler named Charles (5+1+1). In Roman numerals, when you are one short of a key number, you place a **I** in front of it, so the fourth Henry becomes Henry IV, and the ninth Louis becomes Louis IX.

To test your understanding of Roman numerals, how would you write the number for the:

Eighth Boniface _____   Year you were born _____

Third Richard _____   The present year _____

Sixteenth Louis _____

Table of Contents

The Roman Empire in its Glory

People could travel in safety in the Roman Empire.

Mighty Rome was buckling under the pressure of barbarians in 476 A.D. How could it happen to a nation once so mighty, so rich, and so well organized? In its days of glory, around 117 A.D., the Roman Empire had extended from northern England across to the valley of the Tigris and Euphrates Rivers, where some of the world's first civilizations were born. The Rhine and Danube Rivers had separated the Romans from the small and primitive Germanic tribes to the north, and the Nile valley was the empire's southern border. The water highway for most of this region was the Mediterranean Sea, which the Romans called *Mare Nostrum* (Our Sea).

But there were land highways as well, and as the saying went, "All roads lead to Rome." The famed Appian Way ran south and east from Rome and connected it with the Adriatic Sea. The Flaminian Way connected Rome with the northeast. Across these water and land highways flowed goods from all over the known world: perfumes and medicines from Arabia, ivory and gold from Africa, furs from the Baltic regions, and food products from all parts of southern Europe. Ships called galleys, powered by wind and slaves, provided goods from exotic places to people hundreds of miles from their source. They also brought people in strange clothing and different shades of skin to the roadways connecting the empire.

Cities were an important part of this vast empire, both as centers of trade and government. Among them (using their modern names) were London in England, Marseille in France, Tarragona in Spain, Carthage in Tunisia, Cyrene in Libya, Alexandria in Egypt, Jerusalem in Israel, Antioch, Tarsus, and Ephesus in Turkey, and Athens in Greece. A new city, which would play an important part in history, developed later. It was Constantinople (now Istanbul), located where the Black Sea connects with the Aegean and Mediterranean Seas.

Much had been gained by having such an empire. People were more secure in what they owned, and as they traveled, they were protected by the Roman army. This period of safety and security became known as the *Pax Romana* (the Peace of Rome). The Roman legions were made up of professional soldiers working under the tight discipline of their commanders. They made fighting a science, and one enemy after another fell to them. However, as the empire increased in size, and serving in the army lost its appeal to Romans, noncitizens were hired to do their fighting for them. These soldiers often had very little loyalty to Rome; they were faithful only to their general.

Another benefit of Roman rule was the common language, Latin, that made it possible for a person from Spain to talk with a person from Turkey. Other languages were also spoken by the common people, but Latin held pretty much the same position in its time as English does today.

Yet, as vast and successful as the Roman Empire was, things were beginning to change. The mighty Rome that once ruled the known world had lost much of its strength by 476 and was easy prey to the barbarians who attacked.

Name _____

Class _____

POINTS TO CONSIDER

1. The Roman Empire was about seven tenths (70 percent) as large as the United States. Why was communication within this area such a serious problem?

_____

_____

_____

_____

2. As a noncitizen who was a merchant in the empire, what would you see as the advantages and disadvantages of the *Pax Romana?*

_____

_____

_____

_____

3. Latin was the common language of that time, and it carried over into English and many other languages. Look in a dictionary that shows the origin of words, and see how many of the first 20 on the page are marked with an "L" for Latin. List them here.

_____

_____

_____

_____

Name _____

Class _____

CHALLENGES

1. What two rivers separated the Romans from the Germanic tribes?

_____

2. What African river valley was at the southern tip of the empire?

_____

3. What body of water was called the *Mare Nostrum?*

_____

4. Name two major Roman highways.

_____

5. What modern English city was called "Londonium" by the Romans?

_____

6. What was the leading Greek city in Roman times?

_____

7. How were Roman galleys powered?

_____

8. What does the phrase *"Pax Romana"* mean?

_____

9. Were most of the common soldiers in the army citizens?

_____

10. What language was most often used in the Roman Empire?

_____

The Roman Empire in Decay

Power struggles between military leaders and emperors lead to instability within the Roman Empire.

As strong as it appeared on the surface, there were trouble spots inside Rome that no one either saw or tried to correct. One was the lack of loyalty many felt toward Rome. Only about 10 percent of the people were citizens; the rest were noncitizen aliens and slaves. As a citizen, a person had special status. When Paul of Tarsus was arrested and was about to be whipped, he told the officer that he was a Roman citizen by birth, and he was immediately freed (*The Bible,* Acts 22). Those without this citizen privilege had no reason to be loyal to the emperor or the nation. They would cause disturbances and occasionally even large rebellions, and the army (whose common soldiers were mostly noncitizens themselves) would be sent to put down the uprising. Lines of men hanging from crosses along the highway told the story of another rebellion that had failed. But it also showed that there were many willing to risk their lives to fight against Roman tyranny.

It cost money to supply soldiers and pay them. Everyone was taxed to pay the cost of an army they did not want in the first place. Government had other expenses as well. The emperors and their high officials lived very well and wasted money on lavish entertainment. Corruption increased the expenses of government, and to pay the bills, Rome put out money that had little value. The poor of the cities could not compete against slaves for jobs, and unless something was done, they might be stirred up to revolt. That could be a serious threat.

To keep the urban poor content, bread and entertainment were provided them. They might go to a chariot race at the Circus Maximus or watch Christians, criminals, and gladiators being torn apart at the Colosseum. Christians were followers of a religious leader from Palestine, Jesus Christ, who had been put to death on a cross by Pontius Pilate. Jesus's followers believed he had been resurrected from the dead by the God of the Jews. Jesus had not been the usual outlaw. He had told stories called parables to country peasants and, according to his followers, had performed miracles. He had encouraged people to be kind and loving, but above all, to obey God. If they did as he commanded, they would meet him in heaven when they died.

Jesus's followers had spread to Rome, and some were servants of the emperor. Unlike the followers of Greek and Roman gods, these people did not treat religion as a ritual observed only on festival days; they were fanatics willing to die for Jesus Christ if necessary. Emperors Nero, Caligula, and Diocletian made life miserable for Christians, but that only made the religion more appealing to many commoners. When Diocletian retired in 305, a civil war broke out. One of those in competition to be emperor was Constantine. According to legend, when he was battling for control of Rome, he looked up and saw a cross in the sky that had these words across it: *"In hoc signos vinces"* (By this sign, you will conquer). He won the battle, legalized Christianity, and, on his deathbed, accepted Christian baptism.

Name _____

Class _____

POINTS TO CONSIDER

1. As a law-abiding noncitizen, how would you react to seeing robbers from your own people hanging from crosses?

_____

_____

_____

_____

2. Would the modern public react any differently to the bloody shows that were put on in Roman times?

_____

_____

_____

_____

3. After doing some reading about Nero and Caligula in an encyclopedia, why do you think Christians were so opposed to them?

_____

_____

_____

_____

Name _____

Class _____

CHALLENGES

1. Of every 10 people in the empire, how many were citizens?

_____

2. How did Paul of Tarsus avoid a whipping?

_____

3. What was the usual punishment for rebellion?

_____

4. Why were most taxpayers unhappy about paying to support the army?

_____

_____

5. Why was unemployment high in cities?

_____

6. How did the government keep the poor happy?

_____

_____

7. Where might a Roman go to see a chariot race?

_____

8. Where might a Roman see gladiators battle?

_____

9. Who were three emperors who abused Christians?

_____

10. Who saw a cross in the sky?

_____

Reasons for the Fall of Rome

It is too simple to say Rome was defeated by the barbarians; it would be more accurate to argue that it was decay within Rome that caused the empire to collapse. By the time of Constantine, the Roman Empire had already lost most of its influence. For administrative purposes, it had been divided into an Eastern and Western Empire, and soon that division became permanent. Constantine created a new capital for himself on the western shore of the Bosporus Strait. This eastern capital was

The greed and laziness of the upper class may have led to the fall of Rome.

soon named Constantinople. The Eastern Empire would last a thousand years, but the Western only another 140 years.

What caused Rome to sink so fast? Historians have argued this for many years, and it is of special concern to major nations who worry about whether they will soon go the way of Rome. These were some reasons:

Social castes were imposed on the people. During the reign of Domitian, it was decreed that the father's occupation would be that of his children. Ambitious people who were poor were stuck and could not work their way up. Lazy people at the top were secure and did not fear losing their status.

Political reasons. Romans ignored their past traditions and concentrated only on the easiest way of governing. They forgot about a Senate that would debate issues and gave the ruler the sole power of authority in all matters. The offices of tribune (who could protect the rights of the poor with a single word, *veto,* meaning "I forbid") and censor (the defender of morals) were forgotten. It was armies, not politics, that settled political issues.

Military reasons. The army became not only a protector against invaders, but a way to gain and hold power. Around the early emperors was an elite group called the Praetorian Guard. If they became unhappy with the emperor they had vowed to protect, they overthrew him.

Most soldiers were not Roman; in fact, the best soldiers were German. These noncitizens were loyal to their general, and if he wanted to challenge the emperor or some other general for control, they did the fighting.

Immorality. The virtues of hard work and self control that had made Rome strong lost out to greed, laziness, and pleasure.

Romans **forgot the past**. They did not know or care about the events that had shaped Rome, and they lost any sense of identity and values. They did not see how the past was affecting the present and how their actions were shaping the future.

The Romans **forgot the bonds** that tied them together as a nation. People were split by class lines between patricians (upper class) and plebeians (lower class), farmers and city dwellers, citizens and noncitizens, army and taxpayers, and between those favoring and those opposing Christianity. It had been said that "the law is the art of the good and the just." Now the law was the tool for greed and corruption that turned the public against their rulers. Groups became so hostile to each other that they could not unite, even against the menace of cruel invaders.

Name _____

Class _____

POINTS TO CONSIDER

1. When the emperor moved to Constantinople, how did that affect the importance of the city of Rome?

_____

_____

_____

_____

2. How might it have helped bring the Romans together if officials like senators, tribunes, and censors had kept their earlier roles?

_____

_____

_____

_____

3. Of those qualities that hurt Rome, which do you think could be the most dangerous for the United States in our time?

_____

_____

_____

_____

Name _____

Class _____

CHALLENGES

1. Where was Constantinople located?

_____

_____

2. Which lasted longest as center of an empire: Rome or Constantinople?

_____

3. How did Domitian's policy hurt those who were ambitious?

_____

_____

4. What Roman official could stop an action by saying *"Veto"*?

_____

5. What official had the power to protect morals?

_____

6. What group of soldiers protected the emperors?

_____

7. Who were the best soldiers in the army?

_____

8. What were the upper class called? _____

What were the lower class called? _____

9. What subject helps a person understand his or her identity and values?

_____

10. Why were the divisions between groups harmful to Rome?

_____

A Mustard Seed that Threatened Imperial Power

Jesus of Nazareth

Who could have guessed that a poor carpenter, with his small group of ordinary people drawn off the streets and beaches of Galilee, could have much effect on anyone? This carpenter, Jesus of Nazareth, told short stories that caught the imagination of the people. One was about a tiny mustard seed that grew into the largest of trees. After his crucifixion on a cross and his burial, his followers were convinced they had seen him alive in person. They fanned out and told others about him. Four writers (Matthew, Mark, Luke, and John) later wrote biographies of him. Luke then wrote the "Acts of the Apostles" about how the message spread.

A convert, Paul of Tarsus, became a missionary traveling to Europe to preach and establish churches. The churches in some cities became especially important and their leader (called a bishop) had influence throughout the area. Peter, the disciple or follower closest to Jesus, became the bishop of Rome, and after he was arrested, he too was crucified (about 66 A.D.). He was not the only victim of Nero's persecution, and hundreds of others were ripped apart by lions for the amusement of the crowds.

Christians and emperors did not get along. Christians refused to consider emperors divine, and since they opposed killing, Christians made poor soldiers. By 300, so many Romans had become Christian that Diocletian, who proclaimed himself to be a god, issued an ultimatum that they either give up their religion or die. A bloody persecution followed, but in the end it was Diocletian who gave up and resigned.

His successor, Constantine, followed a much different policy, and instead of punishing the Christians, he worked with them. In 325, he called a meeting of the church, the Council of Nicaea. The emperor presided at the meeting, even though he was still not a baptized Christian. This event, however, brought the Cross and Crown together as equals. On his deathbed, Constantine asked for and received baptism.

A nephew of Constantine, Julian, became emperor in 361. He was a moral and intelligent young man who had been trained in ancient Greek and Roman culture. He believed in the ancient virtues of courage, justice, prudence, and temperance. He refused to accept Christianity and its virtues of faith, hope, and charity. Julian died in battle while fighting the Persians and was called "Julian the Apostate" (an apostate is a turncoat, renegade, or traitor) by Christians afterward.

In the Western Empire, the bishops were playing a more important role. Ambrose, the bishop of Milan, forced the emperor to do penance (go through punishment) for his sin of massacring a city. When Emperor Honorius moved to Ravenna in 410, the bishop was left as the most important person in Rome. Other bishops began addressing the Bishop of Rome as Pope (the Latin word for father was "papa"). The influence of Christianity had spread across the Mediterranean world.

Name _____

Class _____

POINTS TO CONSIDER

1. How was the early church like the mustard seed in the parable?

_____

_____

_____

_____

_____

2. Do you think persecuting Christians was probably an unwise policy? Why?

_____

_____

_____

_____

_____

3. How would you explain how the Bishop of Rome (the Pope) was able to become the most important bishop of the western church?

_____

_____

_____

_____

Name _____

Class _____

CHALLENGES

1. What four men wrote biographies about Jesus?

_____

2. What book told the story of the early church?

_____

3. What were leaders of important churches called?

_____

4. What title did Peter hold?

_____

5. Who was responsible for Peter's death?

_____

6. What were two reasons Christians did not get along with emperors?

_____

_____

7. What did Diocletian demand of Christians?

_____

_____

8. What church meeting was called by Constantine?

_____

9. What insulting name was given to Julian by the Christians?

_____

10. What title of respect was given by Christians to the Bishop of Rome?

_____

Barbarians at the Gate

Attila the Hun

Around the fringes of the Roman Empire were wild and dangerous barbarian tribes who murdered and stole wherever they went. They were like gangs that come in and take over neighborhoods. The Goths came out of Sweden between 100 and 200 A.D. and gradually split into two gangs: the Visigoths (West Goths) and the Ostrogoths (East Goths). They were tough, savage fighters and hard as nails. The peaceful people either left or paid bribes to the Goths to be left alone.

Then another gang moved into the neighborhood. They were the Huns, who had been forced out of China and had wandered through Russia. About 372, they came into Goth territory. They were so tough that the Goths were forced to retreat into the Roman Empire. The Romans did not want them around and fought a battle with them at Adrianople in 378. The Goths won, settled in the Eastern Empire, and demanded tribute (bribes) from the Byzantine (Constantinople) government.

Other gangs were making misery for the Western Roman Empire. In 407, two Germanic tribes (Vandals and Burgundians) crossed the Rhine River on the ice. They attacked the Roman legions in Gaul (France) and took land for themselves southwest of Paris (now called Burgundy). The Vandals continued into Spain and Africa. Their reputation was so bad that we still use the words "vandal" and "vandalism" to describe property destruction.

The Visigoths also moved in, and in 410 they were looting and burning in Italy. After looting Rome, they raided southern Gaul and Hispania (Spain). The kingdom they established in Spain lasted 200 years. With Roman strength also reduced in England, the native Celts became targets for sea-roving invaders: Jutes, Angles, and Saxons.

Attila became king of the Huns in 434 and tore up northeastern Gaul until the Romans and Visigoths joined forces to defeat him. Stopped there, Attila attacked Italy and headed for almost defenseless Rome. Instead of meeting an army there, he saw Bishop Leo and some other church leaders coming out to meet him. No one knows what happened to change Attila's mind. Perhaps it was the garments of these men, or their holiness, or their courage. Maybe he feared divine punishment for attacking such angelic men. Whatever the reason, he pulled back and moved north to Bavaria, then to the Danube Valley and the region we call Hungary. Attila died in 453, and his followers began withdrawing toward the Volga River. Europe was relieved.

Then the Vandals, who had been in Africa, suddenly attacked Italy in 455, captured and looted Rome, and made themselves at home. Hiding under the pretext that he was acting for the Byzantine emperor, Odoacer, a Germanic chief, carried off the last emperor of the West, Romulus Augustulus, and sent him to a country house near Naples in 476. The barbarians had taken over. The Roman Empire had vanished, but its influence remains in language, architecture, literature, and law.

Name _____

Class _____

POINTS TO CONSIDER

1. As a ruler of either the Eastern or Western Empire, what kind of advice would you be getting on why you should try to keep these barbarians happy?

_____

_____

_____

_____

_____

2. How would you account for Leo's success in handling Attila?

_____

_____

_____

_____

3. With life so insecure, how do you think the people who had been invaded must have reacted to the changing times?

_____

_____

_____

_____

Name _____

Class _____

CHALLENGES

1. Which Goths threatened Constantinople? _____

Which threatened Rome? _____

2. Who came along to make the Goths miserable?

_____

3. Which side lost the Battle of Adrianople?

_____

4. Which tribes threatened the Western Roman Empire?

_____

5. By what name is Gaul known today?

_____

6. What group do we associate with the destruction of property?

_____

7. What leader succeeded in saving Rome from Attila the Hun?

_____

8. What modern nation is named for Attila's people?

_____

9. What barbarian destroyed the last of the Roman Empire in 476?

_____

10. Who was the last emperor of Rome?

_____

Barbarians Take Charge

All over Western Europe life and property were insecure. In England, the Angles and Saxons pressured the Celts in the south, while the Scots and Picts threatened from the north. One legendary Celt leader, Artorius (King Arthur) won battles against the Saxons in the 6th century. A few victories were not enough, however, and the Celts were pushed back into Wales and Cornwall. The Saxon conquerors left their sea-going ways and turned to farming. They carved England up into small kingdoms, but

Barbarian tribes were continually launching invasions into western and southern Europe.

when the Danes threatened in the 9th century, they joined forces under Alfred the Great. He defeated the Danes in 886, then built forts and ships to defend England. The Saxons ruled England until 1066, when Normans, led by William the Conqueror, crossed the English Channel and defeated the Saxons at the Battle of Hastings.

In Italy, an Ostrogoth named Theodoric became the ruler. He admired the ancient Roman traditions and seemed more Roman than barbarian. He encouraged farming and trade and began rebuilding the roads. But the Goths' rule in Italy was brief. The Eastern Emperor, Justinian, succeeded in taking Italy from them in 552; then the Lombards, a fierce German tribe, pushed the Byzantines out in 568.

Most Germanic tribes came like a summer storm, destroying everything in their path, but moving on. One group was different—the Franks. Not much is known about their origins, but there are many legends. In 451, they made their entrance into recorded history as their King Merovich joined the Roman soldiers in fighting the Huns. His grandson, Clovis, far out-shined him and became one of the outstanding people of the Middle Ages.

Clovis was only 15 when he became king. He was ruthless, savage, and cruel. He once killed a man in an argument over a vase. His wife, Clotilda, and his children were Christian, as were some other Franks, but Clovis was pagan. In 496, when a battle was going badly, he vowed he would accept Clotilda's God if He would help Clovis win the battle. After he won, Clovis and 3,000 of his men were baptized by the bishop. His conversion did not improve his character, but it made him an ally of the church, and from then on he protected church property.

Clovis won battles and forced others either to withdraw or submit. He pushed the Visigoths into Spain, and they made Toledo their capital. Frankish rivals were removed through war or murder. He drove the Allemani back across the Rhine River. Much of present-day France and Germany was in his hands. He made an alliance with the Eastern Empire against Theodoric, and the Byzantine emperor named Clovis as a consul.

Clovis had established the Merovingian line (named for his grandfather), but it was not a smooth-running family. When Clovis died, his kingdom was divided among his four sons. They hated each other and were soon at war. This became a family tradition.

Name _____

Class _____

POINTS TO CONSIDER

1. After reading about the Celts, Saxons, and Normans in an encyclopedia, what qualities do you think they had?

_____

_____

_____

_____

_____

2. Why do you think the Eastern Emperor did not want Theodoric to succeed in rebuilding Rome?

_____

_____

_____

_____

3. Clovis was successful, but he was very cruel. Do you think that rulers of that time needed to be cruel to be successful?

_____

_____

_____

_____

Name _____

Class _____

CHALLENGES

1. By what name do we know King Artorius?

_____

2. What Saxon leader defeated the Danes in 886?

_____

3. Who led the Normans against the Saxons in 1066?

_____

4. What Goth became interested in rebuilding the Roman economy?

_____

5. Who was the first Frankish king we know by name?

_____

6. Why did Clovis convert to Christianity?

_____

_____

7. What happened to the Visigoths after Clovis defeated them?

_____

_____

8. What two modern nations were part of Clovis's territory?

_____

9. How did the Byzantine emperor reward Clovis for fighting Theodoric?

_____

10. What happened to Clovis's kingdom after he died?

_____

Islam: a New Threat to Europe

To Europeans, it must have seemed that every disaster that could happen had already happened: Goths, Huns, Lombards, Franks, and other travelers had dropped by, taken what they wanted, and destroyed everything else. Then came the pressure of a new religion that was spreading rapidly: Islam.

Its founder was Mohammed, a camel driver and traveling merchant who had been born in the Arabian town of Mecca. There were 300 gods honored by the people in this

The Islamic religion spread from Arabia, across North Africa, and into Spain.

town. As Mohammed talked with Jews and Christians, he was convinced there was only one God, whom he called Allah. His public attacks on the pagan gods created enemies for him since Mecca was a center for pagan worship, and in 622 A.D. he escaped the city with his family. This event was "Year One" for the Moslem (Islamic) faithful, and his escape from Mecca to live in the city of Medina was called the Hegira (flight). His teachings were written in the Koran *(Qur'an).* He taught that there was a special place in heaven for those who died for their faith. When the leader (caliph) called for a Holy War *(Jihad),* the loyal follower's duty was to respond.

Islam was like a mighty sword, cutting its way across the Middle East. By 639, the region from Iraq across Egypt was Moslem. Then it continued across North Africa. The Byzantines tried to stop the Moslems from taking any more of their land in Africa and were defeated in 640 at Heliopolis. In 711, the Moslems crossed from Africa into Spain; the Pillars of Hercules were renamed the Straits of Gibralter in honor of a Moslem general. On the other side of the Mediterranean, the Moslems besieged Constantinople; the Eastern Empire was in danger of extinction. The siege failed, but in Spain, the Moors (as the Spanish Moslems were called) wiped out the old kingdom of the Visigoths and crossed the Pyrenees Mountains into France. They conquered southern France and were advancing on Paris. If they succeeded in destroying France, then conquering Europe was certainly a real possibility.

Charles Martel (The Hammer) rose to the occasion and defeated the Moslems at the Battle of Tours in 732. The Moslems were pushed back across the Pyrenees Mountains into Spain. The Moors built a kingdom in Spain that lasted until 1492, the year Columbus sailed.

At first, the Europeans looked upon the Moslems as more barbarians, but in truth, the Moors were to play a valuable role in the future of Europe. While others ignored the literature of the Greeks, the Moors preserved it. The Moors had high regard for Aristotle and referred to him simply as "the Philosopher." As practical people, the Moslems valued the insights of those with whom they came in contact. They expanded on the mathematical work of Ptolemy and Euclid. Their medical schools taught the importance of cleanliness, diagnosis, and the uses and effects of drugs. Our language still uses many of their terms: alcohol, algebra, zero, etc. Their navigational instruments would be important to sailors who traveled beyond sight of land in later years.

Name _____

Class _____

POINTS TO CONSIDER

1. After reading about Islam, Judaism, and Christianity in an encyclopedia, what teachings are similar to all of them?

_____

_____

_____

_____

2. What was there in Islamic teachings that made Moslems especially hard to defeat on the battlefield?

_____

_____

_____

_____

3. How much easier did the Moors make it for Christian Europe to become more skilled in medicine and exploration?

_____

_____

_____

_____

_____

Name _____

Class _____

CHALLENGES

1. What was Mohammed's occupation?

_____

2. Who convinced him there was only one God?

_____

3. Why was he forced to flee from Mecca?

_____

_____

4. Where does the "Year One" begin in the Moslem calendar?

_____

5. What was a Jihad?

_____

6. By what name are the ancient "Pillars of Hercules" known today?

_____

7. Who stopped the Moslem advance into France?

_____

8. What happened to the Moors after that?

_____

_____

9. What Greek philosopher was especially admired by the Moors?

_____

10. What did the Moors learn about medicine that we still think is important?

_____

Charlemagne Rises Above the Rest

Charlemagne

There was little that was royal or majestic about the Merovingian rulers of France; they were either fools or corrupt. Outside help was needed to run their affairs, and they relied on the "Mayor of the Palace" (a chief administrator). The most powerful person was often someone other than the king, a person like Pepin, Charles Martel's son, or Boniface, Archbishop of Mainz. Pepin and Boniface went to the Pope and asked if the person who *really* ruled should be the king. The Pope sided with Pepin and in 754 crowned him king. Pepin "the Short" was a fine king, moral and wise, much better than the Merovingians who preceded him.

When Pepin died in 768, his two sons, Charles and Carloman II, became joint rulers; three years later, Carloman chose to retire to a monastery, so Charles ruled alone. At that time, he was only 26 years old. Much of his next 46 years would be spent fighting 50 campaigns against Germanic enemies. He also helped the Pope against the Lombards who threatened Rome. Loyal to the church, he demanded that the Saxons he defeated in Germany either become Christians or die. Most chose to be baptized as Christians. Some stubbornly refused to convert. Charles, a man of his word, beheaded 4,500 of them at the same time.

In Rome, Pope Leo III was attacked and left for dead by a group of rowdies. After Leo's wounds were bound, he was taken to the camp of Charles, who was nearby. The Frankish army restored order and helped Leo return to the Lateran Palace. The next Christmas, in the year 800, while Charles was attending church in Rome, the Pope placed a crown on his head and proclaimed him "Emperor of the Romans." Charles was now so powerful that he was known as Charlemagne (Charles the Great).

Charlemagne not only knew how to win battles, he knew how to rule. He divided his empire into counties. The head of civil government was the "count," and in each county, there was a bishop or archbishop in charge of the churches. The county's main landowners met several times a year to pass laws and act as a court. The king sent special agents *(missi domenici)* to check on local officials and make sure they were not taking bribes or abusing the people. Charlemagne was concerned about education and brought a great scholar in to teach his children.

Much taller than the average man of his time (6'4"), he was well built and kept himself in good shape with exercise and moderation in food and drink. He had four wives during his long lifetime, and they produced 18 children. He was a good father who enjoyed his family. Charlemagne enjoyed music and singing. He hoped to learn to write and practiced holding a pen. In case the skill should come in the middle of the night, he slept with paper under his pillow and a pen by his side. He developed interests in science, law, literature, and religion. His reign brought a degree of civilization to Europe that had been missing since before the invasions had begun.

Name _____

Class _____

POINTS TO CONSIDER

1. Why do you think Charlemagne came down so hard on the pagan Saxons?

_____

_____

_____

_____

2. In what ways did Charlemagne bring order to France?

_____

_____

_____

_____

3. Do you think Charlemagne would make a good leader for a modern nation? Would you vote for him for president? Why or why not?

_____

_____

_____

_____

Name _____

Class _____

CHALLENGES

1. Who ran the kingdom for the Merovingians?

_____

2. Who persuaded the Pope it was time for a change in France?

_____

3. How did Charles come to rule alone?

_____

4. What choice did Charles offer the Saxons?

_____

5. Who crowned Charles "Emperor of the Romans"?

_____

6. What name was Charles later known by?

_____

7. What two officials were most important in a county?

_____

8. What was the job of the missi domenici?

_____

_____

9. How many wives did Charlemagne have during his life? _____

How many children? _____

10. What were Charlemagne's interests?

_____

The Viking Plague from the North

It seemed that whenever Europe was about to settle down and the people could enjoy safety and prosperity, some new group came along to make life miserable. Shortly after the death of Charlemagne in 814, a new and frightening threat came to loot and destroy. There was no trouble recognizing them. They wore layers of animal hides and leather helmets and carried round, wooden shields. Their long, wooden ships, with a snake or dragon head on the prow and single sail, moved swiftly to attack and then

The Vikings were fierce, seafaring warriors from Scandanavia.

left quickly after they had robbed and burned. Of all the invaders who had attacked Europe, they were the most feared. The people prayed: "God, deliver us from the fury of the Northmen."

Scandanavia was home to the Vikings, and they were ancestors to the Swedes, Norwegians, and Danes. At home, they lived in small villages, grew crops, and raised livestock. Their villages were well organized and were governed by a council *(Folkmoot)*. It was the *Folkmoot*, not a king, who made the decisions for the community. It decided when they would go to war. It seems the Vikings loved the thrill of war more than any other people in history. In battle, Vikings often used a two-edged sword and aimed at the enemy's arms and legs. They also used a broad axe, arrows, and spears. Their most fierce warriors were the *berserkers,* who prepared for battle by eating wild plants and other foods that drugged them and made them crazed.

The Vikings were pagan worshippers of the gods Odin and Thor. Odin was the god of battle and death. Thor ruled the sky and controlled the storms and winds. At sea, Thor helped them more, but when they landed, Odin became the more important god. They attacked in small raiding parties; small seacoast towns, churches, and monasteries were favorite targets.

There were no sailors as daring as they, and their explorers set out for distant places. They reached Iceland in 870; Eric the Red landed in Greenland in 982. About the year 1000, Eric's son, Lief Ericson, landed on the North American coast, found wild grapes, and named his discovery Vinland.

An attack on Dublin in 795 was followed by plundering raids along the coasts of Ireland, western England, France, Germany, and eventually as far south as Sicily. Overland raids from Sweden spread into Russia and down the rivers to Baku on the Caspian Sea and Istanbul (Constantinople) on the Black Sea. By about 875, some Vikings continued to raid, but others were ready to settle down. A group of Danish Vikings, called Normans, settled on the coast of France (Normandy). With William the Conqueror as their leader, they attacked and defeated the English in 1066.

The Vikings would eventually establish peaceful kingdoms in the Baltic area. They became Christian and began to fit in better with other Europeans. But in general, the turmoil they created was harmful to the peace of others. People turned to local leaders to protect them. This led to the system of feudalism that dominated Europe for many years.

Name _____

Class _____

POINTS TO CONSIDER

1. Do you find it odd that a group could be law-abiding at home and wild men when they traveled to another place?

_____

_____

_____

_____

2. What skills did the Vikings have that other sailors of the time did not have?

_____

_____

_____

_____

3. What advantages did settling down offer to the Vikings? What did they give up as a result of becoming peaceful?

_____

_____

_____

_____

Name _____

Class _____

CHALLENGES

1. How did the Vikings decorate their ships?

_____

_____

2. What modern nations had their beginnings with the Vikings?

_____

3. Who among the Vikings made the decision to go raiding?

_____

4. Who were the fiercest Viking warriors?

_____

5. Who were the two most important Viking gods?

_____

6. What targets did they especially like to raid?

_____

7. What Viking explorer reached North America? _____

What did he call it? _____

8. What Danish Vikings settled on the west coast of France?

_____

9. Who led the army that invaded England in 1066?

_____

10. What system developed in Europe as the result of Viking raids?

_____

Feudalism Comes to Europe

The lord's castle, where vassals could seek protection, was usually in the center of the feudal manor.

Imagine that you live in an area where there are several hills. The people live in great fear of what the people on the next hill might do to them. They are hungry and tired, so they find a leader, and they promise him that if he will protect them, they will serve him the rest of their lives. As long as they are near the hill, they feel more secure, but they dare not travel beyond that hill. They become suspicious of outsiders, fearing strangers are trying to find a way to attack them. A few merchants may come with goods to sell, but how will they pay for the goods?

What would happen to trade in the downtown area? How would they eat? What would they wear? The people would have to produce everything themselves, wouldn't they? Since they could not get to outside goods, and goods could not get to them, they would have to learn to make their own. If you can imagine this, then you can understand the feudal system.

The *vassal* (the one who wanted the help) came to the *lord* (the one who could give the help), and in return for protection, food, and clothing, the vassal would be the lord's servant for the rest of his or her life. The nobles were vassals of the king; the peasant was vassal to the nobleman. The king had authority over the nobles, but could not give orders to the peasant, who was the noble's servant. The exception to that rule was in England. The land the noble received from the king was called a *fiefdom.*

If you were my vassal, what kinds of power did I have over you? I would have *military power* over you. I could expect you to fight for me. If I were the one attacked, you would serve without pay for as long as necessary. If I were the one attacking, then you would be my soldier for six weeks; after that, I would have to pay all your expenses. Even when there was no war, I could call on you to guard my castle occasionally.

Political service. If I wanted you to come to my castle for your advice on any subject (war, marriage, or anything else), you must come. I could also expect your *financial help* if I were going to fight a crusade or get married. When your father died, then you would have to pay for the right to continue as my vassal. If you were a girl, then you would need my permission to marry. You would also need my approval to give any land to the church.

If I failed to protect you as I promised, then you could protest to my lord (if I had one). If I were the king (and had no lord), then you might ask for the help of someone strong enough to oppose me. If they succeeded in defying me, they would become your new lord and protector. If you did not live up to your obligations, I could try you in a court made up of my other vassals. If you were found guilty, you would have to surrender your fiefdom.

Wars were common, but there were rules against fighting from Friday through Sunday, from Thursday through Sunday of Holy Week (Easter), and on certain holy days. There was usually no fighting during the winter or harvest. These limits helped reduce the violence.

Name _____

Class _____

POINTS TO CONSIDER

1. What were some conditions of the time that kept anyone from getting very rich?

_____

_____

_____

_____

2. Who do you think got the better end of the deal: the lord or the vassal? Why?

_____

_____

_____

_____

3. What can you see in the qualities of the feudal system that made wars more likely?

_____

_____

_____

_____

Name _____

Class _____

CHALLENGES

1. What title was given to the person who asked for protection?

_____

2. What was the title given to the person who did the protecting?

_____

3. What did the person who asked for protection have to do?

_____

_____

4. Who would be the lord of a nobleman?

_____

5. Could a king in France order the peasant of a nobleman around?

_____

6. If the nobleman received land from a king, what was the land called?

_____

7. If your lord were fighting a defensive war, how long were you required to serve him?

_____

8. How would a vassal who did not live up to his obligations be tried?

_____

_____

9. How many days a week, at most, could combat take place?

_____

10. What seasons were ordinarily not used for fighting?

_____

Showdown at Canossa

The feudal system created complicated arrangements between lords and vassals. Added to those problems were relations between king and church. What if the vassal was a bishop who controlled church lands? Who should appoint that bishop: the king as his lord or the Pope as head of the church? These were important issues when nobles became bishops in order to control church land; the church became a major land holder within a kingdom. During the Middle Ages, the church held about one third of the land in Europe. Kings insisted that the bishop or abbot (head of a monastery) was a vassal, and he should receive the symbols of that office from

Pope Gregory VII

the king (lay investiture). Church reformers did not like this because they felt it divided the loyalty and duties of local church officials.

The modern person usually sees the Pope as a holy man, devoted to serving God and the church. In the early Middle Ages, the Pope had a different image. At first, the Popes had been appointed by the clergy (priests) of Rome and nearby regions, but then the German nobles began choosing the Pope. In 1059, the College of Cardinals was formed by high church officials around Rome to select future Popes.

Pope Nicholas I (858–867) had tried to bring all clergy under the control of the Pope, but after he died they returned to ignoring the Pope's orders. With churchmen practicing simony (buying and selling their positions), the Pope's control was very weak. Reformers met at Cluny, France, and demanded an end to church corruption. They wanted the Pope to control the church. Kings, they said, should have no power to choose church officials.

A leader in this reform movement was Hildebrand, a high Roman Church official. In 1059, he was elected Pope Gregory VII by the cardinals and began making changes. In the future, no priests could be married, and the Pope would choose the bishops. If the Pope made a decision, only the Pope could change it. Gregory's claim of more papal authority was bold and was not going to be popular among the rulers.

The Holy Roman Emperor, Henry IV, was furious with Gregory and insultingly called him a "false monk." In 1077, after a clash over the choice of an archbishop, the Pope excommunicated (expelled) Henry IV from the church. No Christian would have to obey the king, and he could lose his throne. Henry crossed the mountains and went to Canossa where Gregory was staying. The king stood barefoot in the snow three days begging for forgiveness. At last, Gregory forgave him.

Henry returned to Germany, where he won the support of the nobles, but clearly was not humble to the Pope. In 1080, Gregory excommunicated him again, but this time it didn't work. Henry brought an army into Italy. Gregory was chased out of Rome, and Henry appointed an antipope (one installed as a rival to the real Pope). Bitter to the end, Gregory's last words were: "I have loved righteousness and hated iniquity. Therefore, I die in exile."

Name _____

Class _____

POINTS TO CONSIDER

1. Do you agree with Gregory that priests should not be married? Why or why not?

_____

_____

_____

_____

2. Would you have sided with Gregory or Henry on the issue of whether kings should have had some say over who would be a bishop? Explain your answer.

_____

_____

_____

_____

3. What advice would you give Gregory and Henry about how to deal with a person you are having trouble with?

_____

_____

_____

_____

Name _____

Class _____

CHALLENGES

1. What was the ceremony called when the lord gave the symbols of office to a vassal?

_____

2. Who selected Popes in the early days of the church?

_____

3. What group was formed in 1059 to select future Popes?

_____

4. What was simony?

_____

_____

5. Where did reformers meet to discuss church corruption?

_____

6. Who was selected as the new Pope in 1059?

_____

7. Whom did the Pope feel should choose new bishops?

_____

8. What ruler disagreed and insulted the Pope?

_____

9. What did the emperor do to gain forgiveness?

_____

_____

10. What is an antipope?

_____

Great Minds in the Dark Ages

St. Thomas Aquinas

The Middle Ages are sometimes referred to as the "dark ages" because education was very limited, people knew little about the outside world, and war seemed to be more important than ideas. Yet, even under the worst situations, there were people who continued to think and began to affect the way others thought. We will not go deeply into their teachings, but will look at some of what they added to the way we think today.

St. Augustine (354-430) was born in North Africa and grew up lazy and wild. His mother prayed that he would shape up, and when he was 33 and living in Milan, Italy, he did. Augustine returned to North Africa, sold his inheritance, and gave the money to the poor. He saw life as two sided: the "City of Man" (human society) and the "City of God" (spiritual world). He thought about war and concluded that war is permitted if it is the last resort and is fought for a just cause. The most glory, he wrote, goes to the one who ends war. His most famous book is *The City of God.*

The Venerable Bede (673-735) was an English priest and scholar. He was much more interested in learning than in attaining status and turned down the offer to be an abbot because it would have interfered with his studies. He had many interests: languages, astronomy, mathematics, and music. One of his accomplishments was devising the formula to decide when Easter should fall each year.

Peter Abelard (1079-1142) was a well-known teacher in Paris, and students came from many nations to attend his classes. He had strong opinions on many subjects and was often in trouble with the church. His most famous work was *Sic et Non* (Yes and No), which debated both sides of issues. He wrote: "By doubting, we are led to inquiry; from inquiry, we perceive the truth."

St. Thomas à Becket (1118-1176) was archbishop of Canterbury and a longtime friend of King Henry II of England. The king wanted to limit church power, but Becket defended the church. When government officials tried to seize church lands and some of the bishops agreed to it, he excommunicated them all. The king was very angry with him and privately complained about this troublesome man. Four of Henry's barons who overheard his complaints went to Canterbury and killed Becket in the cathedral. The public was so outraged that the murderers were forced to go to the Holy Land for 14 years, and the king, who denied responsibility, allowed himself to be flogged at Becket's tomb.

St. Francis of Assisi (1182-1226) gave away his riches and lived as a beggar preaching to the poorest people in the cities of Italy. He loved nature and found God revealed in every living thing. He believed everything that God had created was for the good of man.

St. Thomas Aquinas (1225-1274) became a monk against the wishes of his family, and his brothers even held him prisoner in a castle for a year. His main interest was theology (the study of God), but he also developed new approaches to thinking, and he believed that the people should participate in government. His views were helpful to democratic thought later on.

Name _____

Class _____

POINTS TO CONSIDER

1. Would you agree with Augustine's views on war? Why or why not?

_____

_____

_____

_____

2. If the king did not order the murder of Becket, do you think he was responsible for it and deserved to be punished? Explain your answer.

_____

_____

_____

_____

3. In what ways were these six men modern in their thinking?

_____

_____

_____

_____

Name _____

Class _____

CHALLENGES

1. What did Augustine do to prove that he had changed?

_____

_____

2. Under what circumstances did Augustine think war was justified?

_____

3. What scholar developed a table showing when Easter comes each year?

_____

4. What was Peter Abelard's profession?

_____

5. What was unusual about *Sic et Non* in its time?

_____

_____

6. Did Abelard think doubt was bad?

_____

7. What was the argument between Henry II and Becket about?

_____

8. How did Becket die?

_____

_____

9. Which of these men was most concerned about nature?

_____

10. Why is Thomas Aquinas of interest to modern people?

_____

Monks and Hermits Reject the World

Franciscan monks belonged to the order established by St. Francis of Assisi

The Medieval world was a terrible place, full of violence and sin. For some people, there was too little of the virtues taught by the Old and New Testament writers. Fear had caused some early Christians to hide away in deserts or on mountainsides. They were called hermits. One lived in the desert for 90 years. The most famous hermit, St. Simeon Stylites, lived on a 60-foot-tall pillar for 30 years. St. Anthony was an Egyptian Christian who lived on a mountain near the Nile River around 300 A.D. He gathered other hermits together in groups of two or three, and they would all come together for worship. These were the first monks. In the difficult times of the Middle Ages, more people wanted to escape from the wars so they could live a quiet life of books and prayer.

The temptations of the world bothered some who feared they might not live a good enough life to reach heaven. Some moved to remote places and lived as hermits, and others moved to monasteries (for men) or convents (for women). After a year of probation, they would join the order and agree to live by its rules. They had volunteered to live with hard work, simple food, and isolation from normal family life.

About 529, a hermit named Benedict started a monastery on a mountaintop in Italy (Monte Cassino). This was the first of many Benedictine monasteries. Benedict wrote tough rules for his monks. The first rule was total obedience to the abbot (head of the monastery). The monks could own nothing (even their clothes belonged to the order). Their workday began at 6 a.m. and continued until sunset; then they ate supper and went to Vespers. At 2 a.m., they went to a prayer service. Their days were spent doing manual labor, copying manuscripts, and praying.

In the 1200's new orders of monks formed: Franciscans, Dominicans, Carmelites, and the Augustinian Hermits. Besides monks who lived away from the world, there were now friars, members of the order who lived out among the people. Each order was easily identified by their cloak, and each had different virtues they stressed. These groups often disagreed over religious issues and became rivals for public support.

Women might join convents (also called nunneries) that followed strict rules similar to the monasteries. Their orders often had the same names as the men's: Benedictine, Dominican, Augustinian, and Franciscan orders of nuns. In the early days, nuns were more free to leave the convent, but later in the Middle Ages they were usually required to stay inside its walls.

A monastery might start with a few monks who lived by the strict rules of the order, but when donations of land and money came in, they often began to change. As vassal to a lord, the abbot became involved in politics. With greater wealth, the order could afford more luxuries, which made the lifestyle more appealing. Enforcement of rules grew lax in time. This led to criticism and demands for reform. Still, in the important areas of education, care of the sick, and safety for travelers, monasteries provided a valuable service.

Name _____

Class _____

POINTS TO CONSIDER

1. What do you think were the main reasons that men and women became monks or nuns during the Medieval period?

_____

_____

_____

_____

2. What were the drawbacks of being a monk or nun that might have prevented you from joining an order?

_____

_____

_____

_____

3. Do you think it was the hermit or the monk who lived the most holy life? Why?

_____

_____

_____

_____

Name _____

Class _____

CHALLENGES

1. Why was St. Simeon Stylites unusual?

_____

2. Who created the first monastery?

_____

3. What were "monasteries" for women called?

_____

4. What was the first rule of a Benedictine monk?

_____

5. How long was the workday at a Benedictine monastery?

_____

6. Name four new orders founded in the 1200s.

_____

_____

7. How could you tell which order a monk belonged to?

_____

8. What other name was used besides "convent"?

_____

9. Why did monasteries become political?

_____

_____

10. What areas of Medieval life were made better by the monasteries?

_____

Rulers with "Uneasy Heads"

Feudal kings were in constant danger of losing their crowns and kingdoms.

When the Vikings were raiding France in 912, King Charles tried to bribe a Norman chief named Rollo with land in northern France. Rollo accepted, which made him the king's vassal. Feudal tradition required that the vassal kiss the lord's foot, but Rollo refused to do it and ordered one of his men to do it for him. The man obeyed, but as he knelt and kissed the king's foot, he raised it so high that Charles tipped over.

The more intelligent feudal kings knew that when the nobles were rebellious they could easily overthrow the king, and all his robes, thrones, and crowns would be of little use. Shakespeare wrote in his play, *Henry IV,* "Uneasy lies the head that wears a crown." As modern observers, we might think that "the King's word is law," but while it was more true in later years, in the Middle Ages, defying the king was more ordinary than obeying him.

In France, that was true for King Hugh Capet (987-996). The Count of Paris, Hugh was chosen by the great nobles of northern France to be king. Every French king down to Louis XVI was related to Hugh Capet. However, Hugh found that his title didn't help much. He had no national army and no national tax sources. In southern France, the nobles barely recognized that he was king and had no intention of obeying him. On one occasion, Hugh got into a bitter argument with a count who was his vassal. Hugh yelled: "Who made you a count?" The count shouted back: "Who made you a king?" It would take many years before French kings began to get respect.

England was developing a degree of order before the Normans arrived. Their system of money was already in place. The first English coin was the "penny," and 240 pennies weighed a "pound." The "shilling" was one twentieth of a pound (12 pennies). In the county or shire, courts were held with important local citizens and royal officials debating and deciding issues. In such an orderly society, the king's role should have been simple. It was not.

King Stephen (1135-1154) was a good example of that. His cousin, Matilda, had a better claim to the throne than he did, but Matilda was unpopular, and a woman, so the nobles swore allegiance to Stephen. He was kind and very likeable, and the nobles took advantage of him. They ignored the law against nobles building castles, and soon many forts went up in England as protection, not against invaders, but to defy royal authority. Matilda was in France plotting against Stephen; when she had enough support, she marched on London and captured him. She ruled as "Lady of England," but was so cruel the nobles turned against her, put Stephen back on the throne, and put her in prison. Finally, she escaped to France.

The Germans had no king. Their dukes were too strong for anyone to rule over them. If they were not fighting each other, they sometimes invaded Italy and drove the Pope from Rome, installing a new Pope in his place. When that happened, some German dukes would side with the old Pope, and some Italian nobles would support the new Pope causing much turmoil. In 962, a German duke, Otto I, was crowned Holy Roman Emperor by the Pope. The title meant little among the German nobles, but was worn by a German nobleman until the 19th century.

Name _____

Class _____

POINTS TO CONSIDER

1. What do you think Shakespeare meant with his statement: "Uneasy lies the head that wears a crown"?

_____

_____

_____

_____

2. What did the count mean when he said: "Who made you king?"

_____

_____

_____

_____

3. What skills do you think it took to be an effective king in those times?

_____

_____

_____

_____

Name _____

Class _____

CHALLENGES

1. How did Hugh Capet become king?

_____

_____

2. Why did Hugh have trouble making the nobles obey?

_____

_____

3. Where did the word "pound" come from as a unit of British money?

_____

4. How many shillings made a pound?

_____

5. Why did Matilda think she should rule England?

_____

_____

6. What was a sign of the nobles taking advantage of Stephen's easygoing nature?

_____

_____

7. What happened after Matilda returned to England?

_____

_____

8. What caused the nobility to return Stephen to the throne?

_____

_____

9. What happened to Matilda?

_____

_____

10. Who was the first Holy Roman Emperor? _____

The Nobility of Europe

Below the rank of king and queen were many "nobles" wearing titles of rank. A title might have a different meaning in another country, but the ones which you will most often see in books include the following. A *prince* is the son of a king; the daughter of a king is a *princess.* Following these, the order of rank was duke, marquis, earl or count, viscount, and baron.

Duke—In England, the duke ranks just below a prince. A member of the king's family was a "royal duke." In some European countries, a duke governed a province or duchy. The wife of a duke was a *duchess.* A *marquis* [pronounced MAR-kwis] was originally an officer in charge of defenses along the marches (frontier regions of the kingdom), but the title became a rank of nobility. His wife was a *marquise* [mar-KEEZ]. In England, the titles were marquess [MAR-kwis] and marchioness [MAR-shu-nis]. *Earl*—In England, this was a rank equal to a

A typical member of the nobility dressed in fashionable court attire.

count on the European continent. The earl's wife was addressed as *Lady. Count*—A title used on the continent; in some countries a count was a member of the royal court, and in others, he was the king's ruler in a district. His wife was a *countess. Viscount* [VIE-kount]—An English officer who acted as a substitute for the earl. Later, it became an honorary rank, and the actual duties went to the sheriff (acting as the substitute for the king). His wife was a *viscountess. Baron*—A major vassal of the king or a person who had given major military service. The wife was a *baroness*, and the children were *baronets.* In 1611, King James I of England created an order of hereditary knights also called *baronets.*

Being a nobleman was hazardous to one's health. These were violent times, and from youth, the sons of nobles prepared for the life of a warrior. They fought wars with outsiders, and if none were available, they fought each other. Wearing a suit of armor or chain mail, with a helmet on their heads, they were in modern terms "one mean fighting machine."

Nobles built high forts for protection and surrounded them with moats (trenches filled with water). These forts were designed more for protection than comfort. The attacker used catapults and battering rams to attempt to make a hole in the wall or gate. Ladders would be used to climb over the walls. The defender used a variety of weapons: boiling water, rocks, and arrows would be used against the attackers.

Arguments were frequent among the nobles, and ways to settle those disputes in court were developed. In Germany, the accused was guilty unless proven innocent. One way to find the truth was *trial by ordeal* in which the accused picked up a red hot iron and carried it a few paces. If his hands healed in the required time, it was proof he was innocent. There were also *trials by combat* in which the two parties fought each other.

Violence requires some justification, or the person is considered nothing more than a murderer or robber. To protect against the Vikings or some other barbarian threat was certainly justification for their existence, but after the invaders left or settled in, the fighting men looked for other reasons to do what they did best. They found these excuses in defense of the church, in the code of chivalry, and in the noblest of all causes: the crusades.

Name _____

Class _____

POINTS TO CONSIDER

1. To what extent do you think modern people are concerned about their prestige?

_____

_____

_____

_____

2. Do you think there are people today who enjoy fighting? Give examples.

_____

_____

_____

_____

3. Do you think the modern soldier has the same qualities as did the Medieval nobility? Explain your answer.

_____

_____

_____

_____

Name _____

Class _____

POINTS TO CONSIDER

1. Why does knighthood seem so exciting and glamorous to the modern person?

_____

_____

_____

_____

2. What was there about being a knight that might make a man into a better person?

_____

_____

_____

_____

3. How would you, as a knight, react to a life without wars?

_____

_____

_____

_____

Name _____

Class _____

CHALLENGES

1. Who used knights to fight the Moslems?

_____

2. What was the main purpose for having knights?

_____

3. What did a student knight do in his first days of training?

_____

_____

4. What lessons in manners were part of the training?

_____

5. What two saints were important to the image of a knight?

_____

6. What order of knights during the Crusades was made up of Frenchmen?

_____

7. What was the most international order of knights during the Crusades?

_____

8. What was the advantage of a crossbow against a knight on horseback?

_____

9. What was the best strategy in fighting a knight?

_____

10. What happened to the use of knighthood as a way to improve a poor boy's status in life?

_____

_____

Ladies of the Court

In a society like that of the Middle Ages, where does the woman fit in? If the chief activity is war, and the woman is not a warrior, then what does she do with her time? If the main part of the household work is done by women of the lower class, what does the "lady of the manor" do?

The modern woman would have difficulty understanding the Medieval woman. She was an inferior. Her status was set by the teachings of Aristotle (who believed women and slaves were naturally inferior), by the statement of St. Paul (that women were to keep silent in the church), and by Germanic laws (that treated women as their husband's property).

When looking for a wife, the nobleman was less concerned with love than in finding a woman who could benefit him, either financially or politically. Couples were often married after their families had bargained a long time over the amount of dowry the bride's father must pay. Sometimes, the couple never even met before they were married. The whole courtship and wedding ceremony took place through letters and contracts.

In southern France, a much more romantic approach to courtship developed in the 11th century. The roving troubadour would sing and play for the woman and win her love. Stories told of the knight who would slay dragons or win contests for the woman in his life, who was not always

In addition to domestic and childrearing duties, noble women were often left to tend to the business of the castle while their husbands were away.

his wife. The romantic tale of Sir Lancelot and Queen Guinevere gave the court of King Arthur the secret love and complications of Medieval romance that are typical of today's soap operas.

Once married, her husband was, in theory, the woman's lord and master. All of her property belonged to her husband, and he could use it or waste it as he saw fit. In practice, she ran the household and supervised the spinning, weaving, and cooking. When the husband was away, she became outdoor supervisor, and if the castle were attacked while her husband was away, she commanded the defense.

The system was against them, but women did not always play the lowly servant's role. When Norman men invaded England in 1066, some of their wives protested when they stayed away too long and warned that if they did not come home quickly, the women would find new husbands. The men said farewell to their army and went home.

Some women were blunt in expressing their opinions. Isabella, the Countess of Arundel, clashed with King Henry III and told him bluntly that he did not govern himself or the nation well. Then as now, wives were not always obedient and silent. Couples that never argued were so rare in England that a couple could win a side of bacon if they could swear, after a year of marriage, that they had never quarreled.

Other women were more subtle. They followed the advice of a character in Chaucer's "Clerk's Tale." "The best way to rule a man," they were told, "was to give him what he pleased." Clever women did exist, and some used Chaucer's advice well in their dealings with men.

Name _____

Class _____

POINTS TO CONSIDER

1. Is there a difference between what laws say and what people do? Give examples.

_____

_____

_____

_____

2. Do you think that the road to success depends on the person you marry? Why or why not?

_____

_____

_____

_____

3. Between 0 as a complete slave and 10 as totally free, where would you put the Medieval woman? Explain your answer.

_____

_____

_____

_____

Name _____

Class _____

CHALLENGES

1. How did Aristotle's opinion hurt women?

_____

_____

2. What was St. Paul's statement about women?

_____

_____

3. What was the role of the woman in Germanic law?

_____

4. What would a nobleman look for in a wife?

_____

5. How romantic was courtship among the nobility?

_____

6. What did troubadours do?

_____

7. What romantic relationship did people associate with King Arthur's court?

_____

8. What was the attitude of Norman women in 1066?

_____

_____

9. What was the effect of their threats?

_____

10. What did Chaucer think a woman could do to rule a man?

_____

The Byzantine Empire is in Trouble

The Hagia Sophia, built in Constantinople during the height of the Byzantine Empire, was completed in 537.

In comparison with feudalism in the West, the Eastern Empire (also called Byzantium) was orderly and strong. Constantinople was ideally located for defense. It was surrounded on three sides by water, and high walls were built along the only landward side. Its army was one of the best in the world, and its navy was strong. Financially, the Empire was in good shape. It was at the crossroads of trade between East and West, and merchants in the city were safe and prosperous. The government was very efficient and operated the same regardless of who was emperor.

The legal system of Byzantium went back to Justinian (527-565). He wrote *Corpus Juris Civilis* (The Body of Civil Law), and it gave all decision-making authority in government to the emperor. "The emperor alone can make laws," said Justinian. The emperor also had the power to decide how the laws should be interpreted. Residents of Constantinople could consider themselves lucky when compared to the confusion in the Western end of the old Roman Empire.

However, there were serious threats to this "good life" in the Eastern Empire. One was that there were no lines of succession to the throne. This was called the "Malady of the Purple" (so called because the emperor wore a purple robe). In the West, heredity was the main determinant of the next king; the eldest son of the king was next in line. But in the Byzantine Empire, any nobleman might decide to replace a dying emperor.

Like the West, the East was threatened by invaders. Slavic tribes came in the 6th century and settled in isolated areas. The Bulgarians came out of Finland and occasionally raided the empire. The Petchenegs and Russians sometimes attacked the frontiers in the 7th century and, a few times, had to be driven from the walls of the city.

The Eastern (Orthodox) Church had little to do with the Roman Church. The most important person in the Eastern Church was the Patriarch of Constantinople, and like the Western Church, there were archbishops and bishops in major cities. But there were differences. The Orthodox baptized by immersing the individual three times. Also, it was required that bishops be unmarried (celibate), but married men could be priests. In 1054, a representative of the Pope (a legate) had been refused when he tried to see the Patriarch. Each church had then accused the other of heresy (violation of Christian doctrine) and broke all ties with each other.

By 1081, the Byzantines were in desperate trouble. The new emperor, Alexius I, faced attack by Turkish pirates from the sea and the vicious Petchenegs from the north. To save Constantinople, he melted down church treasures to pay another group of Turkish people to support him. Still, the Moslems kept coming, and Alexius panicked. He desperately turned to the Pope for help. Gregory VII could not respond; he was too busy fighting off Henry IV. Pope Urban II, who followed, saw some advantages in going to the aid of the Eastern Empire. It would unite Western Christians in a common cause, strengthen the image of the Pope as leader of the Christian world, and might bring the Eastern church under the control of the Western church. He decided to call for a Crusade.

Name _____

Class _____

POINTS TO CONSIDER

1. Do you think that Constantinople's location and wealth might have been a problem for it? Why or why not?

_____

_____

_____

_____

2. Do you think that kings should have been chosen on the basis of family ties or merit as a leader? Explain your answer.

_____

_____

_____

_____

3. If you were Alexius I, why might you hesitate to invite the Roman Church to come to your rescue?

_____

_____

_____

_____

Name _____

Class _____

CHALLENGES

1. Why was Constantinople important in world trade?

_____

_____

2. Who wrote Byzantium's legal code?

_____

3. Who made the laws for the Eastern Empire?

_____

4. What happened when an emperor died?

_____

_____

5. Who were four groups of invaders that threatened Byzantine territory?

_____

6. What title was given to the head of the Eastern Church?

_____

7. What were the rules about marriage in the Eastern Church?

_____

_____

8. When did the Eastern and Western Churches break relations?

_____

9. Who asked the Pope for help?

_____

10. Which Pope decided to help?

_____

"God wills it!" The First Crusade

In 1095, Pope Urban II traveled north to Clermont, France, and gave a speech to the church leaders and nobles who came to hear him. It was one of the most dramatic speeches in history. He called on the descendants of Charlemagne to rescue their fellow Christians in the East and the holy city of Jerusalem from the Moslems. He told them to forget family and possessions and their past feuds and wars and take up the Cross for the holy cause. He also promised them everlasting life in heaven if they went. The people cried out: "God wills it! God wills it!" Their symbol was a cross worn on their tunics. "Crusade" literally meant "to take the cross." The message spread quickly as leaders spread the word.

The cross became the symbol of the crusaders as they journeyed to Jerusalem.

Peter the Hermit was a preacher who rode around France on his donkey. His sermons caused commoners to leave their work and follow his banner to free the Holy City from the Moslems. Five divisions of commoners were formed in April 1096 and started east. The first two were led by Walter the Penniless, and they arrived in Constantinople in mid-July; the others arrived two weeks later. They were weak, tired, and hungry at the end of their journey. They crossed the Bosporus to Asia Minor (Turkey) in August and were wiped out by the Seljuk Turks who left their dead bodies to bleach in the sun.

The knights had gathered separately and were led by Godfrey, Bohemund, and Robert. Some traveled to Constantinople by land, others by sea. Their motives for going varied from those going for purely religious reasons to those planning on using this as an opportunity to get rich quick. The leaders were divided and jealous, each often working against the others. Fortunately for the crusaders, their Moslem opponents were also badly divided and plotting against each other.

In 1099, the crusaders captured Antioch after a long siege. Just after they captured the city, they were surrounded by a newly arrived Moslem army. When the situation was at its worst, a warrior found what was said to be the lance that had pierced Jesus's side. This was seen as a sign that God was with them; the crusaders rallied and fought their way out. They marched on to Jerusalem, where they easily overcame the resistance. Once in the city, the crusaders slaughtered 10,000 Jews and Moslems. Godfrey was offered the title of "king," but took a more modest title: "Defender of the Holy Sepulcher." Three other kingdoms were established at Antioch, Tripoli, and Edessa.

These kingdoms, known as "crusader states," were not very strong and depended heavily on Italian merchants who used their harbors for trade. After the Moslems captured Edessa, the Second Crusade began. Its two leaders, Conrad III of Germany and Louis VII of France, did not work together, and when the crusade failed, they went home in 1148. A new threat to the crusader states came in the form of Saladin, a great military leader. In 1187, he captured Jerusalem and took its king as a prisoner.

Name _____

Class _____

POINTS TO CONSIDER

1. What argument would have persuaded you to go on the First Crusade?

_____

_____

_____

_____

_____

2. Alexius was not pleased when he saw the large numbers of Western Europeans coming to Constantinople. Why do you think that was?

_____

_____

_____

_____

_____

3. What do you think might explain the massacre of Jews and Moslems that occurred when the crusaders captured Jerusalem?

_____

_____

_____

_____

_____

Name _____

Class _____

POINTS TO CONSIDER

1. What other legendary characters besides Robin Hood have you heard of that might or might not have been real persons?

_____

_____

_____

_____

2. Diplomacy is skill in handling rulers of other countries. How would you rate Richard in that department?

_____

_____

_____

_____

3. Why do you think Richard has always been so popular when he accomplished so little?

_____

_____

_____

_____

Name _____

Class _____

CHALLENGES

1. Name three rulers who went on the Third Crusade.

_____

_____

2. What legendary character do we associate with Richard?

_____

3. Who were Richard's parents?

_____

4. Whom did the English clash with at Acre, besides the Moslems?

_____

5. Who was the sultan of Egypt?

_____

6. How many times did Richard try to capture Jerusalem?

_____

7. Where was Richard captured as he traveled home?

_____

8. Who demanded a ransom for Richard's return?

_____

9. How much ransom was demanded?

_____

10. What did Richard do after he returned to England?

_____

The Crusading Spirit Declines

Enthusiasm for crusading came like a gale at times, then dropped to a quiet breeze almost as quickly. These later crusades often had more of a gangster than a religious motive to them, and none came out as planned.

The Fourth Crusade (1202-1204) was called by Pope Innocent III, but was used by the Venetians, who transported the 12,000 crusaders, to attack Zara (a port belonging to the Christian ruler of Hungary) and Constantinople. The crusaders never went beyond the Byzantine capital, and their behavior everywhere they went was an em-

Children believed their innocence would bring them victory, but their crusade ended in tragedy.

barrassment to the Pope. He did what he could to stop them from their cruel deeds, but even the threat of excommunication had no effect.

The Children's Crusade (1212) ended in disaster for those who joined. In Germany and France, children were caught up in the crusading spirit; they believed that in their innocence they could accomplish what the older crusaders could not. Led by a peasant boy named Nicholas and encouraged by their parents and some priests, many children joined the banner. Many died while trying to cross the Alps, and others who managed to get to the ships were taken to North Africa and sold as slaves.

The Fifth Crusade (1217-1221) was fought to conquer Egypt. After the Egyptians lost the Battle of Damietta, they offered to trade Jerusalem for Damietta, but the crusaders rejected the deal. After losing the battle for Cairo, the crusaders were forced to trade their lives for Damietta. There were no battles fought on the Sixth Crusade (1228-1229), but Emperor Frederick II got Jerusalem from the Moslems through diplomatic means. The Seventh Crusade was led by King Louis IX of France. He was captured, and the French nation had to pay a large ransom to get him back. After he returned to France, he attacked Tunis (in North Africa), which began the Eighth Crusade (1270). This effort was also a failure; after he died during the siege, the crusaders returned home. That was the end of the crusades.

Several important changes occurred as the result of the crusades. (1) They were the first united effort of Western Europe. (2) The religious motive was a far more noble cause than the greed, ambition, and revenge that were usual reasons for fighting. (3) They stopped the Moslem expansion that threatened to overwhelm Europe. (4) They increased the power of kings, since many of their more powerful vassals were away. (5) They hastened the rise of cities since the feudal lords needed the cities' help to finance their trips. (6) They improved relations between lords and peasants and tended to unite the society. (7) Europeans became more familiar with geography, not only of the Mediterranean region, but their own countries. (8) Europeans became aware of new products, new methods of farming, and the writings of Greeks and Romans that had been long forgotten in Europe. (9) Europeans discovered that the Moslems were not idolaters or barbarians. Their scholarship was superior to that of Europeans, and Europeans became aware of how much they had to learn. (10) On the negative side, the idea that religious wars were pleasing to God caused the bloodshed and persecution of small minority groups in Europe.

Name _____

Class _____

POINTS TO CONSIDER

1. After looking at all the crusades, do you think they ever really had a chance of driving the Moslems out of the Holy Land? Why or why not?

_____

_____

_____

_____

2. Do you think that the average crusader was in it to get rich, or do you think there were other motives more important to him? Explain.

_____

_____

_____

_____

3. Why do you think there was no Ninth Crusade?

_____

_____

_____

_____

Name _____

Class _____

CHALLENGES

1. Whom did those on the Fourth Crusade attack?

_____

2. How did the Pope try to stop the crusaders?

_____

3. Why did young people leave home to join the Children's Crusade?

_____

_____

4. What happened to the children?

_____

_____

5. What city was captured by those on the Fifth Crusade?

_____

6. What happened to the city after the Battle of Cairo?

_____

7. Which king started the Seventh Crusade?

_____

8. What happened to him?

_____

_____

9. What city were the crusaders trying to take on the Eighth Crusade?

_____

10. What caused it to end without success?

_____

A Legal System Develops in England

An early English law court.

In many parts of Europe, rulers could do whatever they liked. If they wanted property, they took it. If someone argued with them too much, that person was tried for treason in a king's court, and if found guilty, he was hanged (if a commoner) or beheaded (if a nobleman). There was little effort made to decide who was innocent and should be freed, or who was guilty and deserved punishment.

In England, by the 13th century, some interesting changes were being made in law that had a great effect on the legal systems used later in the United Kingdom and the United States.

By the time Henry II became king in 1154, civil and criminal law had already been split. Civil law usually involves an argument over property, and the court's role is to be an umpire. For example in the case of *Smith v. Jones,* Smith is the plaintiff (the one who claims to have been wronged), and Jones is the defendant (the one accused). The court decides if Smith has a legitimate complaint. Criminal law covers actions by an individual that the government says cannot be allowed. In the terms of that time, the action violated the "king's peace." The punishment under criminal law for violating the "king's peace" was fine, imprisonment, or death. Henry ordered that every county have a jail.

The jury of that time was much different than our juries today. In 1166, Henry II ordered that each sheriff appoint 12 good men out of every 100 to be jurors. The jurors of that time investigated rumors they had heard about a local person who, for example, was stealing chickens. If they were convinced the person might have done it, the jury ordered the sheriff to arrest that person and bring him before the judge. These charges were called "presentments." In the 13th century, a second jury was formed; it was called a petit (petty) jury, and it, rather than a judge, decided guilt or innocence. However, most trials were decided by a judge.

Another of Henry's major changes was developing common law. It was so-named because law was intended to be the same in all of England. When a judge wanted to decide a case, he looked up opinions that had been given by judges in similar cases. If the judge saw something similar, but his case involved other facts that were different, he wrote up his opinion. At the end of a year, these opinions were gathered in the "Year Book."

Having men trained to deal with common law cases was necessary for the system to work. This training was provided in Gray's Inn, Lincoln's Inn, or the Inns of Court. Students read during the day and, at night, argued practice cases in "moot" trials. Three languages were needed: Latin for the official records, English to talk with the client, and Norman French for the courtroom. When the student was ready to argue a case in court, he was "called to the bar." Much of what we in America and England know as our law system goes back to ideas present around the year 1200.

A Legal System Develops in England

Name _____

Class _____

POINTS TO CONSIDER

1. Would you feel more comfortable having your case heard by a judge or by a jury? Why?

_____

_____

_____

_____

2. How does the job of a modern juror differ from that of a juror in the time of Henry II?

_____

_____

_____

_____

3. What skills were required of a lawyer at that time?

_____

_____

_____

_____

Name _____

Class _____

CHALLENGES

1. What are most civil cases about?

_____

2. Who brings the case to court in a criminal case?

_____

3. In the case of *White v. Black,* which one is being sued?

_____

4. What were the punishments in criminal law for breaking the "king's peace"?

_____

5. What was the duty of a juror in the early days?

_____

_____

6. What were the charges brought against a person by the jury called?

_____

7. What is the duty of a petit jury?

_____

_____

8. Where did a judge go to find out what previous judges had decided?

_____

9. What were moot trials?

_____

_____

10. What languages did a lawyer need to know?

_____

King John Signs the Magna Carta

King John

For all of his brilliance in creating a justice system for England, Henry II had a blind spot when it came to family matters. He put his wife, Eleanor of Aquitaine, in prison, and she got revenge by stirring up their sons against Henry. Richard and John plotted with the French King Philip Augustus against Henry. Henry had never liked Richard, and of his sons, John was clearly the favorite. After Henry's death, Richard (the Lion Hearted) became king. While he added little to the monarchy, he did nothing to tear down the improvements that his father had made. In 1199, Richard died, and John succeeded him.

John was an evil man and violated nearly every principle of justice his father had created. He wanted his nephew's land; he stole it, and the nephew suddenly disappeared. He fell in love with a 12-year-old girl who was engaged to one of his vassals. John married her despite public protests. John had a bitter argument with the Pope and was excommunicated. That should have cost him all support, but he threatened to punish nobles if they obeyed the Pope. John locked up a noble lady and her son and then allowed them only a piece of raw bacon and uncooked oats to eat; they soon died. Stories spread about a Jew in Bristol who refused to pay a special tax. Each day a tooth was knocked out until he gave in on the eighth day. John's unpopularity among the common people was so great that the commoners began to look to the barons for relief.

The nobility were complaining even more than the commoners. They began to gather around Stephen Langton, the Archbishop of Canterbury, who openly criticized the king. John had pressured the barons to help him invade France; when most had refused to go, he hired professional soldiers (mercenaries) and raised taxes on the nobles to pay for them. The war went badly, and finally the nobles decided it was time to act.

On June 12, 1215, the barons rode out to a meadow along the Thames River called Runnymede and met King John. They brought a document with their demands on it, and after a week of debate, John put his seal to it (he did not know how to write). This document is known as the Magna Carta (the Great Charter). There were 63 points in it, many of which involved trivial subjects. However, there were major points as well. Every person was entitled to justice, and only those who knew the law and obeyed it should be made officials. The king was to refund illegally collected fines and grant a general pardon.

Two parts of the Magna Carta were especially important in the long run. The 12th article said there must be no tax levied unless by "common consent of our kingdom." This led to "no taxation without representation." The 39th article provided that no freeman could be tried except by the "lawful judgment of his peers." The only "freemen" were nobles, but out of this grew our jury system. Now, government was more limited in what it could do.

Name _____

Class _____

POINTS TO CONSIDER

1. Do you think John helped or hurt himself by his acts of cruelty? Why?

_____

_____

_____

_____

2. Since King John, no English ruler has called himself John II. Do you think that has been by coincidence or is there a reason for it?

_____

_____

_____

_____

3. If the Magna Carta had been the last words ever written on reform, would it have made any difference in the long run? Why or why not?

_____

_____

_____

_____

Name _____

Class _____

CHALLENGES

1. Who was Henry II's favorite son?

_____

2. Who preceded John to the throne?

_____

3. After John was excommunicated, what did he do?

_____

_____

4. Whom did the unhappy nobles turn to as a leader?

_____

5. Why were the nobles especially unhappy with John in 1215?

_____

_____

6. What do the words *Magna Carta* mean?

_____

7. How did the king "sign" the Magna Carta?

_____

8. What qualities did the writers of the Magna Carta want in royal officials?

_____

_____

9. What modern phrase comes from the "common consent" clause?

_____

10. What part of our legal system came from the "lawful judgment of his peers" clause?

_____

Castles and Forts Give More Power to the Nobility

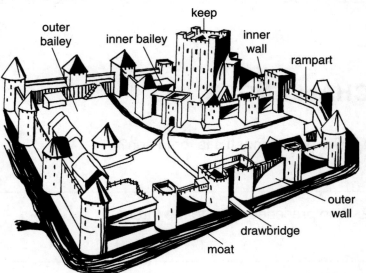

A typical medieval castle

(Labels on illustration: outer bailey, inner bailey, keep, inner wall, rampart, outer wall, drawbridge, moat)

The conflicts between King John and his nobles were also common on the continent. Evidence of that is still seen in Europe. On steep hillsides and mountains, there are tall towers to remind us of the Middle Ages, when wars were as common as the rain, and lords built castles for defense. We have all seen these in movies and television shows. Some castles were very elaborate, whereas others were plain and might even be high piles of earth flattened on the top. Why were they built, and what were they like?

Castles were built so the nobility and the rich could feel safe from other lords and from the commoners. There were few signs of the "homey touch" about them. The inside walls were stone, and the only decoration was usually a tapestry (to provide a little color and to cut down on the draft). Outside, the castle was built to discourage unwanted intruders. Safety, not style or comfort, was the most desired quality. The castle had to be able to withstand an attack or a siege. In a siege the enemy would surround the castle and wait for the defenders to be weakened by hunger or thirst, so it was necessary that castles not only be solidly built, but also provide space for food and water to be stored and livestock to be kept during sieges.

To give some idea of their design, imagine we are vassals of Prince Charming. His beautiful girlfriend, Cinderella, has been kidnapped by the cruel Baron Meanandugly, who has taken her to his castle. Like other castles of the time, this one stands on a high hill, and its tall walls stand 50 feet or so above us, and above the walls are the towers. Armed with a sword or mace (a spiked club), we set out to rescue Cinderella.

As we approach the castle, our first barrier is water. A moat (a ditch filled with water) surrounds the fort, and usually the only way across it is the drawbridge. When the baron sees us coming, he raises the bridge, and we must use our siege machine to cross the moat. We now run into our second problem. The castle is surrounded by two or three short walls. These had been added to the castle's defenses after the crusades. Between the walls are grassy areas (baileys) that are used to graze livestock during a siege. After we cross one bailey with some casualties, the defenders withdraw behind the second wall and inflict more casualties. Finally, we reach the castle's high walls. Our task is even more difficult now.

Some of our men begin climbing ladders up the wall, and as they climb, they are hit by scalding water poured down from the top of the wall. We are also using a battering ram to pound our way through the gate. The enemies stand on walkways (ramparts) and shoot arrows at us. Hanging out over the walls are battlements, which give the baron's men a better angle from which to shoot. We finally break through the gate and find ourselves in the inner bailey, a large courtyard.

Now we come to the strongest defense the baron has—the keep. It is the tall tower where the baron lives. It has its own wells, living quarters for some of his troops, and storage space. Once inside, we must fight our way up the stairs and into the tower where Cinderella is being held. Surviving all this, we might suggest that in the future, the prince lay siege to the castle and just wait out the enemy.

Name _____

Class _____

POINTS TO CONSIDER

1. Why do you think it was more common to lay siege to a castle rather than attempt to scale the walls?

_____

_____

_____

_____

2. Do you think most vassals were enthused about fighting in these wars? What would you have been thinking during this battle?

_____

_____

_____

_____

3. What kinds of food would you have stored in the keep, just in case a siege might occur?

_____

_____

_____

_____

Name _____

Class _____

CHALLENGES

1. What was the most desired quality expected of a good castle?

_____

2. Why were castles built?

_____

_____

3. Why were tapestries hung?

_____

4. What are baileys, and why are they there?

_____

_____

5. What is a moat?

_____

6. What is the purpose of the battering ram?

_____

7. What is the purpose of the battlement?

_____

8. What is the keep?

_____

9. Who normally lives in the keep?

_____

10. How is the keep made self-sufficient?

_____

Cities Grow in Size and Influence

In our society, cities are "where the action is;" they are centers of business, industry, government, professional sports, and the news media. Our view of cities is far different than it was in the Middle Ages. After the Roman Empire fell, there was little need for cities, but when trade began to pick up around 1000 A.D., they began to grow. Medieval cities were far smaller than ours, both in space and population, and were of little importance to most people of that time.

Many cities of the Middle Ages owed much to the Roman era. Paris, for example, had long been inhabited by a tribe

Medieval streets were crowded with houses, merchants' stalls, people, and animals.

called the Parisii and went by the name of Lutetia (Mudtown). The Romans made it part of their road network that tied it to Lyon, Marseilles, and other key points in France. London's history went back to Celtic times, but the Romans called it Londonium. The old Roman town was destroyed by a fire in 1087, but it was quickly rebuilt and became the political center of England. Others were "new" cities. When Kaiserschloss Castle was built in 1050, the town of Nuremburg grew up around it.

Medieval cities all grew up around a castle (called a *bourg*), where residents could escape to in case of attack. The lord who built the castle was glad to have these people around because they could supply him with soldiers in case of war, and whatever they owned could be taxed. As the population grew and became wealthier, the people built walls around the city to protect their property from outside attack. Cities were built near rivers, so drawbridges were built that could be raised in case of war.

These were the Middle Ages, and like everyone else, the residents of the cities were vassals under the rule and protection of the king or a powerful lord. Like other vassals, they had to pay their dues in service. What was different was that the people in cities might tax themselves to pay for the privilege of *not* having to work the lord's land or fight in his wars. If the city was vassal to a king, he usually did not interfere with the details of the lives of its residents, as long as they paid their taxes. The residents could choose their own leaders and make their own rules.

In the center of the city was the marketplace, the ruler's palace, and the cathedral. The city was divided into districts (often 12 districts, to honor the 12 apostles). The pattern was generally circular. At the middle were the homes of the wealthy merchants and local nobility. Near the middle were the work shops, churches, and schools. At the outer edge were the huts of the poor.

Space was in short supply within the city's walls; this caused the streets to be narrow and buildings to be five and six stories tall. After it got too crowded, cities built new walls. Sometimes the old walls were torn down, but in other cases the old walls were kept, dividing towns into districts that separated the classes from each other.

Name _____

Class _____

POINTS TO CONSIDER

1. What causes cities to become more important or less important?

_____

_____

_____

_____

2. What would have impressed you about the city if you had lived on a feudal estate all your life?

_____

_____

_____

_____

3. What might your impressions be of a Medieval city if you were transported back in time to the Middle Ages?

_____

_____

_____

_____

Name _____

Class _____

CHALLENGES

1. What was the original name of Paris, and what did the name mean in English?

_____

2. What did the Romans do that helped Paris become so important later?

_____

_____

3. What was the Roman name for London?

_____

4. Why was the "bourg" important to town dwellers?

_____

_____

5. How did river cities protect themselves from attack?

_____

6. Where did the wealthy residents live?

_____

7. What would you expect to find in the middle of the city?

_____

8. Where did the poor live?

_____

9. Why were new walls built?

_____

10. What happened to the old walls?

_____

Cathedrals: Monuments to Faith

What makes one city different from another? Today, we build stadiums, arches, zoos, and statues for people to see. In the Middle Ages, city leaders also wanted to make their city outstanding. The two ways this was done was by building a magnificent cathedral and a university.

The cathedral was the home church for the bishop or archbishop. It had a special chair for the bishop called a *cathedra.* The early cathedrals were built like the Greek and Roman temples; the structure was as simple as when a child lays a block across two upright blocks. Around the 11th century, the Romanesque style of cathedral came in. It was made of stone, had thick walls, narrow openings for light, and rounded arches. The statues in them had to follow guidelines set down by the church, and no sculptor could show any originality in design.

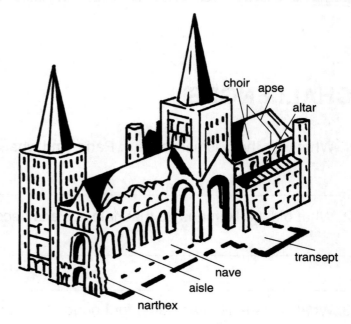

Diagram of a typical cathedral.

During the 13th century, the Gothic style cathedral became very popular in Germany, France, and England. It was spectacular in size, height, and design. Its walls were heavier than any previously constructed; to keep them from collapsing outward, they were supported by flying buttresses. Crowning the work were the steeples and spires, like arrows pointing to heaven. Doors and windows were pointed too, like hands at prayer. The glaziers (glass makers) used translucent glass of many colors, each color significant in meaning. Everything that was done had a symbolic meaning.

The Gothic cathedral was usually shaped like a large cross. A visitor entered through the large doors at the front into the narthex (inside entrance) located on the west side of the cathedral and walked down the nave toward the altar. About halfway down the nave, the visitor saw the arms of the cross (transepts) off to the north and south. Walking straight to the east, the visitor came to the apse, where the choir and altar were.

Cathedrals often took 50 to 100 years to build, and thousands of individuals played a part in their construction. Many volunteered out of community pride and because of religious enthusiasm. Others were paid. The unskilled workers received low wages for the very hard work of cutting stones, moving them to the building site, and setting them in place. Masons cut the stone into just the right size and shape to fit their spot in the building, and the best masons made the statues. Masons were well paid when they were employed. Becoming a mason required seven years of apprenticeship and passing a test. There was always a shortage of masons, partly because those who had the rank did not want too many competitors, and also because so many died of lung diseases caused by the stone dust they breathed.

Most of the great cathedrals built during the Middle Ages still stand, and only war and fire destroyed the others. Experts are divided over which is the greatest. When you enter these massive structures, you see the pride and devotion to detail that made them monuments to faith.

Name _____

Class _____

POINTS TO CONSIDER

1. What do you think motivated the Medieval people to build such large and ornate cathedrals?

_____

_____

_____

_____

_____

2. What modern construction devices would have made cathedral construction easier for the Medieval workers?

_____

_____

_____

_____

3. Why have so few cathedrals been built in the 20th century?

_____

_____

_____

_____

Name _____

Class _____

CHALLENGES

1. Where did the name "cathedral" come from?

_____

_____

2. What style used thick walls and rounded arches?

_____

3. How were the walls supported?

_____

4. What was the shape of the door meant to represent?

_____

_____

5. What were the glass makers called?

_____

6. What part of the cathedral was pointed from west to east?

_____

7. What part was pointed north to south?

_____

8. What part included the altar and choir?

_____

9. How long did it take to become a stone mason?

_____

10. Why were there shortages of stone masons?

_____

Medieval Universities: Centers of Learning

Medieval universities grew from gatherings of students who assembled to hear famous scholars give lectures.

In our time, going to college or a university is common, but there was a time, even in the United States, when colleges were scarce. Harvard, William and Mary, and Yale were the earliest colonial colleges, and their students got heavy doses of Latin and Greek. They were copying the style of English universities of their time, all following traditions of Medieval universities established centuries before. Note taking, lectures, and tests, followed by receiving a diploma and wearing a cap and gown, are present day reminders of those times.

Medieval universities started without a campus. A famous scholar would come to town, and students would come to learn from him. The students sat on the floor or on benches. The teacher lectured, and the students took notes. By the time the course was over, the student had a book full of notes which he either kept or sold to a new student. These notebooks were expensive, and students wrote home to ask their parents for more money. Some things never change! Lectures were all in Latin, and the area of Paris where students lived came to be called the "Latin Quarter." Latin was the universal language of the educated, so no matter which country was the student's homeland, he could converse with the others.

Students varied in qualities and character. Many were very serious and eager to learn. Others were troublemakers who took their university days as a time to party and enjoy life. Wealthy students lived far better than those from poor families, but some aid was available for the poor. Robert Sorbon gave money for a hall in Paris where 16 poor students could live free. The school that developed around that hall came to be the Sorbonne, one of the most famous universities in the world today.

The students in town were easily identified by their scholars' gowns, and they often clashed with the local young people who thought they were snobs and foreigners. Students complained about the prices they were charged for food and lodging. To protect themselves, teachers and students formed guilds (like the craft guilds of the time). These were called *universitas,* meaning "all who belong to the guild." In 1200, students in Paris had a fight with local police, and after some of the students were killed, they threatened to move elsewhere unless they were given the right to be free from local rule. The king gave them a charter saying they were responsible only to church law.

The two main universities at that time were at Paris (famous for its study of theology and philosophy) and Bologna in Italy (famous for its law school). Salerno was becoming famous for its study of medicine.

The young man who successfully passed all the tests was awarded a B.A. degree. If he continued his studies, he could earn an A.M. degree, the minimum requirement to be admitted to the teaching guild at the university level. Doctoral degrees were also conferred on those who could teach law, medicine, or theology. Other doors were open to a young man with university training in the church, government, law, or medicine. For the poor, it was one way to rise above their humble status in life.

Name _____

Class _____

POINTS TO CONSIDER

1. In what ways are schools, colleges, and universities of today similar to those of the Middle Ages?

_____

_____

_____

_____

2. Why would some residents of a university town want the students around and others prefer that they be gone?

_____

_____

_____

_____

3. Do you think a college or university degree is still important for a young person who wants to move up in life? Why?

_____

_____

_____

_____

Name _____

Class _____

CHALLENGES

1. How did a Medieval university begin?

_____

_____

2. What language was used for university lectures?

_____

3. What was the student section of Paris called?

_____

4. What did Robert Sorbon do that made his name world famous?

_____

_____

5. What were common student complaints about their living conditions?

_____

_____

6. What did *universitas* mean?

_____

7. What university became famous for its medical school?

_____

8. What was the best university at which to study law?

_____

9. What degree was granted to the student upon graduating?

_____

10. What were some careers open to university graduates in the Middle Ages?

Life in the Middle Ages: the Cities

As trade began to revive at the end of the 11th century, towns which had been dormant began to develop a new enthusiasm and larger population. There were many reasons peasants might want to move to the city. They could be more free. A person living in a city for a year and a day was free from any previous feudal obligation. They could own land and either rent or sell it. They could learn a trade and possibly even become a leader. Since nearly all cities were located near the walls of a burgh (fort), those who led the local community were known as bur-

Cities became centers of trade and provided opportunities for many lower-class people to earn wealth and respectability.

gesses (English), bourgeois (French), or burghers (German). Many burgesses were from lower-class families, but had become successful in the city.

The upper class in cities lived well. They had large homes with many rooms, glass windows, and carpets on the floor. Their ambitions made them want to marry their daughters off to nobles, so there would be titles of nobility in the family and added prestige. The old aristocracy looked down on burghers and insultingly called them *nouveaux riches* (new rich).

Guilds in the city played an important part. The tailors in the city, for example, formed a guild and blocked anyone who was not a member from selling clothing. Thus, customers received better quality clothes but paid higher prices for clothing because guild merchants could charge more than they might have otherwise. Guild members did not do all the work; they hired others to work for them. The tailors gave cloth to seamstresses to turn into clothes and paid them by the piece. In Florence (Italy), there were seven important guilds and about 15 minor guilds.

Cities were centers of trade as well as production. Part of the business was with local customers, but part of it involved bringing in goods from distant places and sending them on to other trading centers. The Italian cities like Genoa, Venice, and Florence developed large navies and drove competitors off of the Mediterranean Sea.

Along with the growth of cities, came serious problems with overcrowding and sanitation. Medieval cities were filthy. Human inhabitants shared space with rats, fleas, pigs, horses, and oxen. Italian cities were the first to begin to pave streets, but the streets in other cities were either dust or mud. Cities did not have garbage collectors, and people dumped their waste products out their windows. Men walked next to the street to protect the women from garbage dumped out of upper windows. Polluted well water caused epidemics that wiped out whole sections of cities. The rich had room, but the poor lived in overcrowded huts. Contagious diseases spread rapidly in the crowded cities, and when health conditions got too bad, the whole city might move to a new location.

Travelers often criticized cities they visited. Rome was noted for crime, bad food, scorpions, and mosquitoes. A Frenchman warned friends to avoid London because of its degenerates, gambling, belly dancers, and beggars. Despite their problems, cities were an alternative to life as a peasant in the country.

Name _____

Class _____

POINTS TO CONSIDER

1. As a peasant young person of the Middle Ages, would your family have encouraged you to move to a city? Why or why not?

_____

_____

_____

_____

2. Do you think the guilds helped or hurt the other residents of the city? Why?

_____

_____

_____

_____

3. In what ways do you think guilds were like or different from modern labor unions?

_____

_____

_____

_____

Name _____

Class _____

CHALLENGES

1. How long did a person have to live in a city before he was free of all feudal obligations?

_____

2. Why were city dwellers called "burgesses" or "bourgeois"?

_____

_____

3. What was meant by *nouveaux riches?*

_____

4. What were guilds?

_____

5. Why was guild membership important?

_____

_____

6. How many guilds were there in Venice?

_____

7. Why did Italian cities build navies?

_____

_____

8. Why did men walk next to the street?

_____

9. What happened when a city became too unhealthy?

_____

10. What city was noted for its crime, bad food, and mosquitoes?

Life in the Middle Ages: the Peasants' Lot

Hidden away and almost forgotten, the Medieval peasant was at the bottom of the pile. Upper classes rarely mentioned them, and if they did, it was to complain of their smell, ignorance, ugliness, or dishonesty.

We might refer to peasants as one group, but there were differences in status that they understood and separated themselves by. There were four different classes: villeins, serfs, crofters, and cotters. Feudal law most protected the villein because his ancestors had made a contract with a lord for protection, whereas the serf's ancestors in the

Peasants worked the lord's land in return for his protection.

village were made subject of the lord as a group. Serfs were tied to the land, and if one lord took the land away from another, he got the serfs too. Crofters and cotters had no land, but rented their services to nobles or rich villeins.

A peasant worked hard for what little he received. The lands he farmed were not all in one place, but were in strips separated by open fields. It was common for peasants to work in groups, both for the companionship and because with the oxen and heavy plows then in use, it was impossible for the peasant to work alone.

The French peasant complained that the king demanded taxes, the noble paid no tax, the priest demanded his tithe, the merchant needed his profit, the soldier paid for nothing he took, and the beggar had nothing to take. The peasant complained he alone was supporting the king, noble, priest, merchant, soldier, and beggar. He was also at the mercy of these people. If the lord had a bishop as guest, he took up a collection from the serfs, and if for entertainment they rode across his land on a fox hunt, the peasant lost hours of back-breaking labor.

It was in the nature of a peasant to be docile and not cause trouble, but there were occasions when resentment broke out in mob violence. In 1356, French peasants were fed up with the salt tax and revolted in the north and west of France. This was known as the Jacquerie rebellion. Out of it came a demand for the taxpayers to have more say in decisions to raise taxes.

In 1381, England was at war with France, and new tax money was needed to pay for it. The merchants and large landowners were tired of being taxed, so Parliament came up with a head tax, and everyone, except beggars, was forced to pay one shilling. The person with the greatest burden from this tax was the poorest peasant, who did not want to sacrifice his shilling to the king. When collectors were sent to catch tax evaders, rebellion spread. Wat Tyler, a peasant, killed a tax collector and became a hero to the poor. The peasants marched on London, and King Richard II fearlessly rode out to talk with them. The peasants returned home with new respect for the king and many empty promises.

The largest peasant revolt came in Germany in 1524–1525 when peasants and urban workers rebelled over higher rents and losses of privileges. They attacked nobles and wealthy priests. Then the rulers sent in armies that crushed the rebels and put the rebel leaders to horrible deaths.

Name _____

Class _____

POINTS TO CONSIDER

1. Why would a villein look down on a crofter when both were peasants?

_____

_____

_____

_____

2. The modern middle-class American feels the government is always in his pocket. Would his complaint bring sympathy from the Medieval peasant? Explain.

_____

_____

_____

_____

3. Peasant revolts were often bloody affairs threatening order and property. Are you more sympathetic to the peasant or those who put down the revolt? Why?

_____

_____

_____

_____

Name _____

Class _____

CHALLENGES

1. What rank of peasant had the highest status?

_____

2. If land was exchanged between lords, what happened to the serfs?

_____

3. How did crofters make a living?

_____

4. Why did peasants work in groups?

_____

_____

5. Why was a nobleman's fox hunt hard on the peasant?

_____

_____

6. Why were French peasants unhappy in 1356?

_____

_____

7. What was the French peasant revolt called?

_____

8. What tax did English peasants have to pay, and how much was it?

_____

9. How did Wat Tyler become a hero?

_____

10. Who were the targets of German peasant anger in 1525?

_____

Life in the Middle Ages: Recreation

People of the Medieval period, like those before and since, looked for ways to enjoy themselves. For upper-class men, the great entertainments were hunting and hawking. They would ride through fields and forests chasing deer or boars. Hawking was a sport that had developed in Asia and then spread to Rome. Hawks were trained to bring down hares, pigeons, and herons. Women sometimes accompanied men on these hawking trips.

The work of a knight was war, and preparing for war involved hours of practice with weapons, which was not much fun. The tournament was in-

Tournaments were designed for entertainment and practice purposes, but they could be just as dangerous as real combat.

vented to make practice more enjoyable. The contests were with swords and lances, and knights who participated came as representatives of noble families or a region. The competitors and their supporters met in a field on the appointed day, and the fight continued until one had defeated the other. These contests were dangerous for the participants, but they could be profitable. The winner received the horse and arms of the loser.

Jugglers and jesters performed for the wealthy. The jesters were made up in ridiculous costumes and gave witty answers to questions. For their efforts, they received food, lodging, and small donations.

Even for the peasant, there were some activities that brought pleasure. The lord gave dinners for his vassals on certain feast days, at planting time, and when the harvest was complete. Feast days were joyous occasions for the peasants. They gathered at the church for physical contests: wrestling and jumping matches, shooting with bow and arrow, and tugs of war. Plays were performed; they were supposed to be religious, but some got so obscene that the church barred them from the churchyard.

Poaching was also a dangerous peasant sport. The forests were only to be used by the lord for hunting, but peasants in need of food or just wanting the thrill of illegal hunting sometimes went in search of game. If caught, the poacher's foot was cut off.

The poor in cities also had festival days where they had fun at the expense of their betters. The Feast of Fools was celebrated in London with a woman of bad reputation being seated on the bishop's throne in the cathedral. The soles of old shoes were burned instead of incense. A town idiot was given a robe and crown to wear and placed on a throne. He was honored as if he were king for the day by the lower classes. No effort was made to stop these little displays of disrespect; it was recognized as a way to let the poor blow off steam.

Plays were popular and educational. They were used by the church to instruct the public, most of which could not read. There were three types of plays: stories from the Bible (mystery plays), those about saints (miracle plays), and plays where the characters represented certain virtues and vices (morality plays). The stage was often a box, and the play lasted 10 to 20 minutes. Guilds often paid the cost of production and performed the plays.

Name _____

Class _____

POINTS TO CONSIDER

1. The Medieval period was a time of warriors. In what ways did their entertainment imitate the times?

_____

_____

_____

_____

2. Peasants often went to excess during feast days. Why would you expect this to happen?

_____

_____

_____

_____

3. Why were plays centered around religious and moral subjects?

_____

_____

_____

_____

Name _____

Class _____

CHALLENGES

1. What were hawks trained to do?

_____

2. How did tournaments come into existence?

_____

_____

3. How could entering a tournament become profitable?

_____

4. Who were the comedians of the Middle Ages?

_____

5. What were three occasions when the noble fed his peasants?

_____

_____

6. What were some physical events that took place on feast days?

_____

_____

7. Why were plays no longer allowed at some churches on feast days?

_____

8. What was the punishment for poaching?

_____

9. What was used as a substitute for incense on the Feast of Fools?

_____

10. What was the subject of miracle plays?

_____

Life in the Middle Ages: Literature

Dante Alighieri, author of the *Divine Comedy*

What people think about is what they write about. In the Middle Ages, with the emphasis on war, chivalry, and religion, those were the topics for literature. Since so few could read, it is not surprising that best sellers were in short supply. Most of what was recorded were old legends that people felt might be lost unless they were written down. The old Celtic legends of King Arthur, the French tales of Roland; the German stories of Nibelungs, and Norse legends about Beowulf and Vikings were finally put in written form.

Beowulf was one of the earliest stories to be written in English, but the legend was brought to England by the invading Vikings. In *Beowulf,* the hero kills a monster named Grendel, then he has to fight Grendel's mother who is seeking revenge. In the end, Beowulf dies from wounds he receives in a battle with a dragon. The story brings out the admired qualities of loyalty and courage.

The same qualities show up in *The Song of Roland,* which is based on an incident in the Battle of Roncevalles. Roland, the nephew of Charlemagne, faces 100,000 Saracens with his small army, but refuses to ask for help from his uncle. After all of his men have been killed and he is wounded, he blows his magic horn, and his uncle returns to find him dead.

The *Nibelungs* were German "children of the mist" who owned a golden treasure. The plot centers around King Siegfried (who has killed a dragon) and his love for Kriemhild. To win her, he helps her brother win Brunhild, who has vowed she will not marry any man who has not defeated her in combat. The story is long and complicated and features battles and love.

The Norse tales of Viking heroes were written during the 1200s and are known as *The Sagas of Icelanders.* Some of these stories are short, but others are as long as novels.

Geoffrey Chaucer was the greatest English writer of the Middle Ages. His best-known work is *Canterbury Tales,* a story centered around 29 travelers on their way to London who stop at an inn. They decide that to pass the time, each will tell two stories on their way to the city and two on their way home. Chaucer never finished his tales, but gave a useful description of the people of 14th century England. In the tale *Romance of the Rose,* the lover is helped or hurt along the way by such characters as Fair Welcome, Evil-Tongue, and Jealousy.

Dante's *Divine Comedy* was also written in the 1300s, and its story begins with Dante lost in a deep forest. There he meets the Roman poet, Virgil, who helps him find his way through hell, then purgatory. For his journey through heaven to the throne of God, his guide is Beatrice.

In 1455, the Gutenburg Bible was published at Mainz, Germany, on a printing press. William Caxton set up the first printing press in England about 20 years later. Earlier printers had concentrated on books in Latin, but Caxton published books in English. After that, books on subjects interesting to scholars were available, but popular writing was also published. The spread of books and knowledge would speed the process of change.

Name _____

Class _____

POINTS TO CONSIDER

1. What topics would great literature being written today focus on?

_____

_____

_____

_____

2. If the young people in your class were to write the Canterbury Tales, what kinds of stories would they tell?

_____

_____

_____

_____

3. The Gutenburg Bible's publication was one of the most important events in the history of mankind. Why was it so important?

_____

_____

_____

_____

Name _____

Class _____

CHALLENGES

1. What two monsters did Beowulf fight?

_____

2. Whom was Roland fighting at Roncevalles?

_____

3. What did Roland do just before he died?

_____

_____

4. Who were the Nibelungs?

_____

5. Whom does Siegfried love?

_____

6. To win Brunhild's hand in marriage, what must a man do?

_____

_____

7. Who wrote about travelers on their way to London?

_____

8. In what story would you run into characters named Jealousy and Evil-Tongue?

_____

9. Who guides Dante as he makes his way through heaven?

_____

10. What book was the first printed on a printing press?

_____

Life in the Middle Ages: Music and Art

What artists and musicians do is also limited by the interests and tastes of their time. In the modern world, a style of art and music can spread in a very short time. The modern musician can become an overnight sensation and sell millions of albums and tapes in many nations. If a song about dogs sells millions of copies, it becomes a fad, and hundreds of new songs are written about dogs. If the public tires of dogs and goes on to speed boats, then dogs are out, and speed boats are what people sing about.

In the Medieval period, the musician and artist were limited by the tastes and markets of their time. No one enjoys starving, so painters and sculptors had to please those who bought their services: churches, religious orders, and noblemen. Art work was commissioned for both the interior and exterior of buildings. Some painters and sculptors were regarded as masters, and to learn the trade, the beginner studied with a master. Soon the

The artist Giotto created a series of paintings depicting the life of St. Francis of Assisi (pictured above).

masters had many imitators who spread their style, and their style became the fashion for others to copy.

A painter named Cimabue (1240-1302) was the son of a rich noble, but unlike many of his class, he wanted to do something worthwhile with his life. He became a painter, and one of his outstanding paintings of the Madonna (the mother of Jesus) was so famous that the French king came to Florence to see it. Unlike the Madonnas painted before, his had dignity and realism.

More important than his role as a painter was his success in recruiting new talent. Legend tells that Cimabue walked down a road and noticed a boy drawing pictures of sheep on a rock. The boy had talent, and Cimabue made him his assistant. The new artist became better known than his teacher. His name was Giotto (1266-1307). Little of his work has survived intact, but Dante and Petrarch claimed he was Italy's best artist.

Fra (Brother) Angelico (1400-1455) was a painter and Dominican monk who bridged the time between the Medieval period and the Renaissance. His work involved many types of art. He was trained as a miniaturist and learned how to draw precisely, but he could also create large paintings. Among his contributions to art was perspective, the technique of having some figures look more distant than others. Much greater artists were yet to come during the Renaissance, but the later Medieval artists were definitely improving.

The most important music of the Middle Ages was religious. The people of that time were in church very often and wanted music pleasing to their ears. The Gregorian chant was popular with the church; it was sung by a person and a choir without musical instruments to support them.

Around 1100, troubadours began to come on the scene. They were singers of love ballads and were especially popular with women. Their types of songs spread to other lands, and in Germany they were called minnesingers. They created a romantic ideal and described men as the weaker sex in their attempts to win over the women of their dreams.

Name _____

Class _____

POINTS TO CONSIDER

1. How many different varieties of art are present now that were not around in the Middle Ages? What made these new art forms possible?

_____

_____

_____

_____

2. What qualities and abilities do artists need to be successful?

_____

_____

_____

_____

3. Why would the music of troubadours appeal more to women than men?

_____

_____

_____

_____

_____

Name _____

Class _____

CHALLENGES

1. Who were the major purchasers of art?

_____

2. How did a person become an artist?

_____

_____

3. How did a style of art become a fashion?

_____

_____

4. What was unusual about Cimabue's background?

_____

5. Who was the boy genius discovered while he was drawing sheep?

_____

6. What kind of training did Angelico receive?

_____

7. What contribution did he make to artistic style?

_____

_____

8. In general, what happened to the quality of art in the Middle Ages?

_____

9. What kind of music became popular in the church?

_____

10. What kind of songs did troubadours sing?

Life in the Middle Ages: Minorities

While most of the people in Western Europe were white Catholics, there were some among them who were not. We need to keep in mind that our ideas about tolerance and fair play for minorities were not part of the Medieval mind. People who were "different" were seen as a menace, and at times they were treated badly by the majority.

An illustration from a 14th century Bible shows three men following the carriage wearing hats that identify them as members of the Jewish faith.

Most Jews lived in the Middle East, but some had come to Europe. A few were farmers, but most became artisans and tradesmen. The church forbade Christians to lend to each other if they charged interest, so the Jews became bankers. Jewish moneylenders made loans at high rates of interest, not because they were greedy, but because it was almost impossible to collect if a nobleman or bishop refused to pay their debts.

After the First Crusade, anti-Jewish sentiment rose, and Jews became the victims of mob action. The Jews turned to rulers for help and got it, but the rulers charged high taxes for their protection. In 1215, the Fourth Lateran Council of the church required that Jews live in ghettoes, and they were to wear a yellow label. Giving in to public anti-Jewish pressure, England and France expelled Jews in the 1290s, and many migrated to Germany. The transplanted Jews learned to speak German and began combining it with Hebrew words. This new combined language was written in Hebrew script and became the modern Yiddish. Life in Germany was not always safe for Jews, so some departed for Poland and Russia. Conditions there were often no better, and they would later become victims of widespread persecution. Some converted and became Christians, while others followed the teachings of Judah Halevi, who dreamed of the day when Jews could return to Jerusalem.

Spanish Jews, by contrast, were treated well by the Moslems and became skilled government officials, bankers, and physicians.

From time to time, Christian groups rejecting church doctrines came into existence. At first these heresies (heresy is a belief going against the official church doctrine) were not taken seriously because church doctrine was not yet clear. By the 12th century however, church beliefs were more clear, and any opposition to those beliefs was viewed as a serious threat by the church and nobility. The Waldensians were one such opposition group. Formed in the 12th century, they followed Peter Waldo, who believed Christians should give their property to the poor. They often clashed with priests, so they opposed having any clergy. The Waldensians were condemned by church councils and were persecuted, but were never completely destroyed.

Albigensians opposed the Catholic Church, describing it as an "instrument of darkness;" they also were against meat, marriage, and private ownership of property. Pope Innocent III declared a "crusade" against them, and since Albigensians also opposed fighting, they were an easy target for their enemies. They were wiped out by the late 1300s. No one who was different was acceptable in the Europe of the Middle Ages.

Name _____

Class _____

POINTS TO CONSIDER

1. Experts say that Jews contributed very little to life in Europe during the Middle Ages. How would you account for that?

_____

_____

_____

_____

2. Some Jews in the Middle Ages converted to Christianity, but others did not. Why might you have chosen to convert, or why would you have refused to convert if you had been a Jew at that time?

_____

_____

_____

_____

3. What groups like the Waldensians and Albigensians are unpopular in modern society and suffer persecution?

_____

_____

_____

_____

Name _____

Class _____

CHALLENGERS

1. What did most Jews do for a living?

_____

2. Why did they become bankers?

_____

_____

3. Why did they have to charge high rates of interest?

_____

_____

4. When were Jews expelled from England and France?

_____

5. What is Yiddish?

_____

6. Where did Jews live after they were expelled from western Europe?

_____

7. What did Judah Halevi want to happen for the Jewish people?

_____

8. What happened to the Jews who went to Spain?

_____

9. Why were the Waldensians so unpopular with the church?

_____

_____

10. What made it easy to persecute Albigensians?

Life in the Middle Ages: Women

St. Clare of Assisi, who vowed to live in poverty and serve others, started an order of nuns called the Poor Clares.

The Medieval woman was very limited in how she lived her life. From the day she was born, she had a male who told her what she could and could not do. Marriages were usually "for convenience," to gain land or property. Henry VII of England searched for a suitable wife after his first wife died and learned that the widow of the King of Naples was available. He sent three agents to find out if she was healthy, attractive, and had money. Their report indicated that she passed the first two qualifications, but failed the third. He remained a widower.

Sometimes, children were only 4 or 5 years old when they were married. The practice of arranging children's marriages was so common that the church said children in the cradle could not be married. If a woman survived childhood without gaining a husband, her choices were to either get married or go to a convent.

In marriage, the husband ruled the family. On certain days, the wife was required to lie at the husband's feet and beg his forgiveness for anything she had done or had failed to do. Then the children did the same at their parents' feet. Wife beating was common, although some rules said that the beating should be "reasonable." Still, women were important in family life, and in Italy they were a power in the family circle.

Women did much of the work during the Middle Ages. They worked in the fields, the same as the men. They spun cloth and made clothing for the family. Even upper-class girls were taught to spin. Women in Paris held a wide variety of jobs in trade and industry. When their husbands died, women continued to operate the businesses. It was said that in London women played an important part in the city's trade.

While many women of the Middle Ages were as illiterate as their husbands and fathers, some education was available in a few places. One of the most famous love stories of the Middle Ages involved Heloise, who fell in love with her professor, Peter Abelard. Their romance cost him his job, and she was expelled from the University of Paris. Women were barred from attending that university after the scandal. However, women still attended Italian universities, and Maria di Novella became a math professor at the University of Bologna when she was 25 years old.

One of the outstanding women of the 13th century was Clare, daughter of a wealthy noble from Assisi. She heard St. Francis speak and decided to live in poverty. She started the order of Poor Clares, and all who joined vowed to live in absolute poverty. Her firmness was shown when the Saracens attacked the town, and she went to the walls; the Saracens were so impressed by her courage that they left the nuns alone. In the care that they took of patients at the convent hospital and their example of self-denial, the nuns made others aware of their own greed and self-centeredness.

Name _____

Class _____

POINTS TO CONSIDER

1. What were some common practices of the Middle Ages that modern women would not like?

_____

_____

_____

_____

2. What role did women play in the work that was done in the Middle Ages?

_____

_____

_____

_____

3. Why might a woman of that time choose to become a nun?

_____

_____

_____

_____

Name _____

Class _____

CHALLENGES

1. What was meant by "marriages for convenience"?

_____

_____

2. Why did Henry VII lose interest in the widow of the King of Naples?

_____

3. What rule did the church have about the earliest age for a boy and girl to be married?

_____

4. What limit was there on wife beating?

_____

5. What were two cities where women were important in trade?

_____

6. Whom did Heloise fall in love with?

_____

7. What happened at the University of Paris after Heloise was expelled?

_____

_____

8. Which woman was a professor at the University of Bologna?

_____

9. What kind of family did Clare of Assisi come from?

_____

_____

10. What was the most important rule for the Poor Clares?

_____

Life in the Middle Ages: Science

If there was any part of Medieval life that seemed to move backward rather than forward, it was science. The word *science* comes from the Latin, meaning "to know." Science, as we know it, involves observation, experiments, and drawing logical conclusions. The scientist uses information that has been gathered in the past, but he or she checks it out against the latest information. Just because something was written in the past does not give it any more influence than a study of that subject done today.

Alchemists worked in vain to convert other metals into gold, but also learned much about the chemical makeup of many substances.

In the Middle Ages, science fell behind where it had been in the year 200 A.D. Scientists did not observe, they merely quoted what Galen said about medicine (much of which was wrong), or Ptolemy (who said the earth was the center of the universe). Nothing that was written could deviate from church teachings. What passed for science in Europe seems more like magic to us.

Alchemy was one of the sciences of the Middle Ages. Its goal was to turn base metals into gold. Geber, a Spanish alchemist, explained that metals were made up of sulfur and mercury, and if conditions were right, any metal could be converted into gold. The alchemist's problem was to find the exact combination of metals, temperatures, and methods that would produce the most perfect of all metals: gold. When found, the new substance would be the "Philosopher's Stone." If taken as medicine, gold would cure disease and might even give the person immortality. The effort was long and unsuccessful. However, in their experiments, alchemists began to learn more about chemicals.

Many alchemists were foolish dreamers, but some were true scientists. One was Roger Bacon, a 13th century Englishman who became interested in optics, astronomy, mathematics, and technology. Bacon saw the possibility of a lens being used to improve eyesight. He studied explosives and said they created "thunderbolts" greater than those in nature. He predicted that someday ships would sail without the aid of the wind and carriages would be propelled without the use of animals.

Paracelsus was a Swiss-born scientist of the late Middle Ages who gave us our words *alcohol* and *zinc* from his studies. He started out as an alchemist, but his interests broadened into experiments with medicines. He was very outspoken and made many enemies, but others began looking to medicine rather than herbs to cure illness.

While Europeans worried about the Philosopher's Stone, Arab scientists were making progress in many areas. When the Arabs conquered Egypt, they took the Greek records from the library at Alexandria back to Baghdad and translated them into Arabic. They did not stop there, but continued to discover for themselves. An Arab physician, Avicenna, wrote a medical book, *Canon of Medicine,* in which he described the symptoms of diseases like meningitis and tetanus. Another Arab, Alhazen, discovered that we see through the reflection of light from objects into our eyes.

Name _____

Class _____

POINTS TO CONSIDER

1. Was the search for gold through alchemy done just because of a desire to get rich? Explain.

_____

_____

_____

_____

2. What modern means of transportation did Bacon predict would come about because of the power of explosions?

_____

_____

_____

_____

3. Europeans eventually returned to a study of science and had to go to Arabs for information. Why was this hard for them to do?

_____

_____

_____

_____

Name _____

Class _____

CHALLENGES

1. What methods are used in modern science to discover information?

_____

_____

_____

2. Whom did Medieval doctors look to for information?

_____

3. Who said the earth was the center of the universe?

_____

4. What two ingredients (according to Geber) were present in all metals?

_____

5. What was seen as the perfect metal?

_____

6. What was the main gain that came from alchemy?

_____

7. What corrective device that you might wear came about because of Roger Bacon's studies?

_____

8. Who focused on medicines rather than herbs as cures?

_____

9. Who first described diseases like meningitis?

_____

10. What did Alhazan say vision was?

_____

Life in the Middle Ages: Health

In 1524, Erasmus wrote a letter to a friend: "I often wonder and grieve to think why Britain has now been afflicted so many years with chronic pestilence, especially the Sweating Disease...." As we look at health during the Middle Ages, we are surprised that people somehow managed to live to be 30 or 40 years old, living and eating as they did. Cleanliness was not a big concern for them. Baths were taken once or twice a year at most. In castles, bath water and body waste were flushed out into the moat surrounding the castle. The meat people ate was often old and poorly cooked, and vegetables were boiled until little nutritional value was left.

While real medical knowledge was in short supply, many religious orders provided care and comfort in hospitals and leprasaria.

Homes had very poor heating systems and were both cold and smoke-filled. Swiss homes were an exception, and travelers noted that there people did not need hats and coats when they were indoors. The poor had no floors in their houses, but even the rich put rubbish under their floors to insulate them. Straw was strewn to sleep on, and in time, it began to smell. Noxious odors in cities came from open sewers, piles of manure, and garbage tossed on the streets. Lice, flies, mosquitoes, ticks, bugs, spiders, mice, and rats spread diseases, and epidemics were common.

People had no knowledge of medicine and relied on superstition to save them. Gregory of Tours believed that God worked through his saints and trusted St. Martin to cure him. The dust from the saint's shrine solved his stomach problems. Licking the rail at St. Martin's tomb healed his sore tongue. To free a fishbone he had swallowed, Gregory rubbed his throat with a cloth that hung at the tomb. Such "remedies" were not uncommon.

Even when the person relied on "science," his physician was not often reliable. Physicians explained that there were four "humors": blood, phlegm, yellow bile, and black bile. Whenever the person's supply of any of these became too great or too small, he became ill. The doctor's cure involved restoring the balance. The leading medical university of Europe was at Salerno, and even there superstition was a major part of the curriculum. Students were informed that onions cured baldness. If a woman did not wish to have a child, she should wear a red ribbon around her head. However, some sound medical advice was also included. Students were told that eating and drinking should be done in moderation. Experiments began on cadavers (dead bodies) of animals and humans. However, performing surgery was beneath the dignity of a trained physician and was left to butchers and barbers.

The Byzantines were the first to develop hospitals. The first hospitals in the West were places for travelers and sick people to find shelter and food. In the 11th century, monks began to take care of the ill, but their main treatment was spiritual healing. Confession and communion were more part of the treatment than medicine. There were about 19,000 leprasaria (leper hospitals) in Europe in the 13th century.

The European lack of medical knowledge, overcrowded cities, and tolerance of rats was about to contribute to an astounding loss of life in the 14th century.

Name _____

Class _____

POINTS TO CONSIDER

1. People are still looking for unusual cures. What are some that you have heard of? Why do people believe in these unusual practices?

_____

_____

_____

_____

2. What were some of the obvious health mistakes people made in the Middle Ages?

_____

_____

_____

_____

3. We use the terms "hospital" and "hospitality" to mean different things. Were their meanings closer together in the Middle Ages? Explain.

_____

_____

_____

_____

Name _____

Class _____

CHALLENGES

1. How often did people in Medieval times take baths?

_____

2. How long did they live?

_____

3. What impressed travelers about Swiss homes?

_____

4. Where did people sleep?

_____

5. What caused odors in cities?

_____

_____

6. How did Gregory of Tours solve his stomach problems?

_____

7. What were the four "humors"?

_____

8. Why were the four humors important to a person?

_____

_____

9. What was the cure for baldness?

_____

10. What cure did monks have for the ill?

_____

The Black Death

John, the smith, was one of those in the 14th century who began running a high fever and whose lymph glands swelled up in his neck. Jeanne, his sister, began hemorrhaging and vomiting blood. No physician was needed to tell them what their problem was. They had the plague. There was no cure, and their life expectancy was now a few days. After their painful deaths, John and Jeanne's bodies were taken out of the house by one of the city's poor and dumped in an open grave. No one understood why they died, and being commoners, no one cared.

Friars administering the last rites to a victim of the Black Death

To the 20th century witness, their deaths were not as mysterious. The bubonic plague (Black Death) was spread because of the fleas on black rats or from contact with a person who had the disease. Ships carried the plague from the Middle East to Italy in 1347, and it quickly spread to France, Spain, England, and Russia. It killed saint and sinner, poor and rich, male and female, without much discrimination. Because cities were so overcrowded, contact with plague carriers was more common there than in rural areas, but no one was safe.

With no known way to avoid the disease, frightened people began to look for any possible solution. Some joined the flagellation movement and beat themselves until their bodies were black and blue. It was hoped that by confessing their sins and going through this self-imposed torment, God's anger would be satisfied. The movement was finally stopped by Pope Clement VI, who threatened to excommunicate the flagellants. Many rulers refused to permit their ceremonies to be performed in public.

Jews had long drunk water from moving streams rather than wells; in this time of mass fear, some charged the reason for that unusual behavior was that Jews were poisoning the wells. It did not seem to matter that Jews were also dying from the plague. Terrible slaughters of Jews took place in Strasbourg, Mainz, and other European cities.

The houses of the infected were quarantined, and no one was allowed to leave. However, some plague victims managed to escape their houses at night, and officers let them go because they were afraid to touch them.

By 1350, the worst of the crisis was over; by then, between 25 and 33 percent of Europe's population had died in the plague. Some cities were especially hard hit. Florence lost about two out of three people.

There were many effects of the plague. Europe's population was greatly reduced. Feudal obligations ended with the death of the noble and his family. After the plague threat had lessened, those tired of the peasant's life used the opportunity to escape to the cities. Workers received higher wages than ever before, but costs went up too. Many monks and priests had died, and their replacements were of poor quality in comparison with them. It would take centuries for Europe to recover from the plague.

Name _____

Class _____

POINTS TO CONSIDER

1. What modern diseases are counterparts to the plague? How do people react to the victims of these diseases?

_____

_____

_____

_____

2. Imagining that the plague came to your family, how would the family react?

_____

_____

_____

_____

3. Some survivors of the plague years came out ahead, while others lost. Make a list of winners and losers.

_____

_____

_____

_____

_____

Name _____

Class _____

CHALLENGES

1. What plague symptoms did John have?

_____

2. Jeanne had another strain of the plague. What were her symptoms?

_____

3. When did the plague arrive in Italy?

_____

4. Why did the plague spread faster in cities than rural areas?

_____

_____

5. Why did a person go through flagellation?

_____

_____

6. What happened to the flagellation movement?

_____

7. What did Jews do differently from others that caused suspicion?

_____

8. Why didn't officers try to stop people infected by the plague from leaving their homes?

_____

9. About what percentage of the people of Europe died from the plague?

_____

10. How did the plague affect feudalism?

_____

The Beginnings of Parliament

Parliament meetings grew out of the need for the king to consult with his vassals to obtain their advice and support.

We usually do not think of the Middle Ages as being a time when people were democratic, and they were not. Absolutism (unrestricted power) was much more in style. Yet, very slowly, the first tiny steps were being taken toward allowing groups rather than individuals to make decisions.

It was customary under feudalism for the lord to call in his vassals to discuss major problems or ask their permission to raise taxes. These meetings were not on a regular basis, and delegates were not chosen by elections to represent the people. Yet, some produced heated exchanges, with the vassals demanding changes. If the vassals had enough power, the lord had little choice except to agree to their terms.

In Anglo-Saxon England, a council called the Witan existed. It was made up of important leaders of the church and nobility; its purpose was to advise the king and sometimes to act as a court. The Norman invaders brought a similar group with them: the Magnum Concilium (the Great Council). It met three times a year, but was too large to accomplish much, so a smaller group was formed, the Curia Regis (the King's Court). The most important member of the court came to be the king's most important advisor, the "Chancellor." The Court's importance increased when it started handling the king's financial matters. Since a checkered cloth was used to count the money, the one in charge was called the Chancellor of the Exchequer.

In 1258, King Henry III gathered a "parliament" of important officials in London. "Parliament" was a French word meaning to "talk" or "discuss." This particular gathering has been called the "Mad (angry) Parliament." They were furious with the king for letting the Pope and Frenchmen have too much influence. The king was forced to approve the Provisions of Oxford, which placed government in the hands of the nobles. When he tried to back out of the agreement, Henry was captured by his most outspoken critic, Lord Simon de Montfort, in 1264. From then until his death, Henry became a "rubber stamp," approving whatever Lord Simon wanted.

Simon called Parliament together in 1265, and for the first time, citizens of towns, knights, barons, and high churchmen met. Kings could no longer ignore the people. From then on, the people's voices would be heard when laws were being considered.

Heir to the throne, Prince Edward, was also held hostage, but escaped and went on the Seventh Crusade. When he returned in 1274, he was crowned king. He knew that to keep power, he must appeal to public opinion. Faced with many problems—war with France and rebellions by the Welsh and Scots—Edward I convened the Model Parliament in 1295, saying that "common dangers should be met by measures agreed upon in common." High churchmen, nobles, and commoners met, but divided into two houses: the House of Lords and the House of Commons. Parliament would keep that form to the present day.

The Beginnings of Parliament

Name _____

Class _____

POINTS TO CONSIDER

1. Why is the power to tax considered to be so important by Parliament, Congress, and your state legislature today?

_____

_____

_____

_____

2. As a ruler, do you think you would have liked the idea of calling Parliament together? Why or why not?

_____

_____

_____

_____

3. Why was the dividing of Parliament into two houses important for us in the United States?

_____

_____

_____

_____

Name_____

Class_____

CHALLENGES

1. What is absolutism?

_____

2. Why did lords have to call their vassals together?

_____

_____

3. Who belonged to the Anglo-Saxon Witan?

_____

4. Why was the King's Court (Curia Regis) created?

_____

5. What was the job of the Chancellor?

_____

6. What official was associated with a checkered cloth?

_____

7. What was the "Mad Parliament" angry about?

_____

8. What happened to Henry III after Simon de Montfort captured him?

_____

_____

9. Why did Edward I convene the Model Parliament?

_____

_____

10. What are the two houses of Parliament?

_____

The Church and its Critics

John Huss

The Medieval church was very different from the modern church; it was an economic and political power as well as a religious power. It controlled much land in Europe. The church was very wealthy. It used its power to threaten kings. It had a monopoly on religion; nearly everyone (except Albigensians, Waldensians, and Jews) belonged to the church. Often, where there is power and wealth, greedy and ambitious men will use it for gain. This was true of the Medieval church. Rulers wanted their man in as Pope, and if someone else were chosen, they worked to limit the damage that Pope could do. Popes were angered by this attempt to control the church, and Pope Boniface VIII issued a bull (papal statement) called *Clericos Laicos* in 1294 prohibiting lay rulers from taxing church property without the Pope's permission. Edward I of England and Philip the Fair of France began taking protection away from the church, and Boniface backed down.

Boniface's prestige returned during religious festivals held in 1300, and he decided to put the kings in their place with another bull, *Unam Sanctum,* in which he claimed the power to remove any king. He said obedience to the Pope was necessary for salvation. Philip reacted strongly and almost succeeded in taking Boniface as a captive to France. The next Pope, Benedict XI, died within a year, and after much debate, Clement V (1305-14) was chosen as Pope. He moved to Avignon (next to France) and never returned to Rome. Scared by the French king, he reversed *Unam Sanctum.* The English saw him as a French puppet and ignored him.

This began the "Babylonian Captivity" of the church. From 1309-77, the Popes lived in Avignon. When Pope Gregory XI moved back to Rome in 1377, he found the situation there was chaos and wanted to return to Avignon, but he died in 1378 before that was accomplished. The French cardinals left Rome after an Italian had been chosen as Pope, and they elected a different Pope. This split was called the "Great Schism." Now there were two Popes, each excommunicating the other. In 1409, a meeting at Pisa decided neither Pope was valid and chose a third one. The other two did not resign, so then there were three. Finally in 1417, the Council of Constance fired two Popes, the third resigned, and Martin V was named as the new Pope.

As you can guess, this was all very confusing to faithful Christians. Two who spoke up in protest were John Wycliffe and John Huss. Wycliffe (1320-1384) was an Oxford professor who saw the suffering caused by the plague and the Hundred Years' War and felt neither kings nor Popes cared about the people. He argued that man must obey God over king or Pope and that the Bible, not the church, had authority over Christians. In 1382, his followers translated the Bible into English. In 1415, the Council of Constance ordered that his body be dug up and burned.

John Huss (1369-1415) was also critical of the church and was ordered to appear before the Council of Constance. Although he received a promise of safe passage, he was captured and burned at the stake.

Name _____

Class _____

POINTS TO CONSIDER

1. How did the Popes become political footballs? Why aren't they that way now?

_____

_____

_____

_____

2. Do you think the English and other nations were right in assuming that the Pope was just a pawn of the French king? Why or why not?

_____

_____

_____

_____

3. How do you think Wycliffe and Huss were important to the Protestant Reformation that would come in the 16th century?

_____

_____

_____

_____

Name _____

Class _____

CHALLENGES

1. What did *Clericos Laicos* say?

_____

2. How did the English and French kings react to it?

_____

3. Why did *Unam Sanctum* get such a strong response from King Philip?

_____

_____

4. What did Clement V do after he was chosen as Pope?

_____

_____

5. During what time period did the Popes live at Avignon? What was that period called?

_____   _____

6. What was the largest number of people ever claiming to be Pope at the same time?

_____

7. In what year did the confusion end?

_____

8. What was Wycliffe's complaint against kings and Popes?

_____

_____

9. What did Wycliffe's followers accomplish?

_____

10. What happened to Huss at the Council of Constance?

_____

The Hundred Years' War

When a king was vassal to another king, there was sure to be trouble. When they were the kings of France and England, and each was determined to hold on to what was his, it added up to 116 years of trouble. The Hundred Years' War, as it was called, was not continuous by any means; there were long lulls in the fighting and many distractions: revolts, political disputes, and the plague years.

English and French armies clashed in several different battles that spanned 116 years.

There had been bad blood between English and French rulers since the Norman invasion. Each tried to stir up trouble for the other. The English had allies in France opposed to the French king. The French helped the Scots fight the English and stirred up the people of Aquitaine against English rule. In 1337, nine years after Philip VI was crowned the French king, Edward III of England claimed the throne was rightfully his, and the war was officially on. Still, little happened until 1346 when both armies met at Crécy.

The French army was made up of 15,000 Genoese mercenaries (soldiers from Genoa paid to fight). When the battle started, they were tired from an 18-mile march in heavy armor, and adding to their troubles, a heavy rainstorm left their bowstrings wet and nearly useless. The English archers were rested and had kept their strings dry. This battle was especially notable because the English brought three or four small cannons with them. The French troops had never heard the boom of a cannon before and thought that "God thundered." The Genoese survived that, but not the volley of white arrows that hit them like a "snowstorm." Crécy was a great victory for England.

John the Good, who followed Philip to the throne, was determined to stop the raids of the Black Prince (the son of Edward III) and get revenge for the defeat at Crécy. With 60,000 men, John faced an English army of only 10,000 men at Poitiers, but the English position was so strong they defeated the French and captured John. French peasants were required to pay a high tax to ransom the king, and that led to the Jacquerie revolt.

The English also had their troubles. For a time, England seemed to pull together, and national pride ran strong. Then taxes went up, hitting the poor the hardest. Wat Tyler's Rebellion (1381) protested the head tax imposed on everyone over 15. Rioting also occurred in London where the Lord Chancellor, collector of the tax, was beheaded. The Black Death also visited both countries and took people's minds off of war.

Later, Henry V decided that war would bring the nation together again and picked a quarrel with the French. In 1415, at Agincourt, a French army of 50,000 met Henry's army of 7,000 to 8,000 men. Again, circumstances favored the English. A heavy rainstorm made the land over which the French crossed so wet that their horsemen sank deep in it. Henry's men put sharpened stakes in the ground to stop the French cavalry. The bewildered French faced a barrage of arrows and once again suffered a humiliating defeat.

Name _____

Class _____

POINTS TO CONSIDER

1. Are you impressed by Edward III's excuse for a war with France? What arguments would you give for or against it?

_____

_____

_____

_____

2. What were some of the effects of the Hundred Years' War on the poor?

_____

_____

_____

_____

3. Henry V started the final phase of the war to win public support. Do you think other leaders have done the same thing? Give examples.

_____

_____

_____

_____

Name _____

Class _____

CHALLENGES

1. With whom had the French worked to weaken the English?

_____

2. How had the English tried to weaken the French king?

_____

3. What was the excuse used by Edward III to declare war on Philip?

_____

4. What new weapon was used at Crécy?

_____

5. Why did the English archers do better than the Genoese archers at Crécy?

_____

_____

6. Why did John the Good want to fight at Poitiers?

_____

_____

7. What happened to John after the battle?

_____

8. What happened in England as a result of the victory at Poitiers?

_____

9. What caused Wat Tyler's Rebellion?

_____

10. How did the weather help the English at Agincourt?

_____

Joan of Arc Steps In to Save the French

The long war with England had produced only defeat and discouragement for France. The French ruler, Charles VII, was an uncrowned king. The coronation (crowning ceremony) had to take place at Rheims, but it was in English hands. Then a 17-year-old girl came to the French court with a message from God. He had chosen her, she claimed, to drive the English from French soil. It was unbelievable, almost as strange as the events of her young life.

Joan was a peasant girl from a small town, Domrémy, who had not learned to read or write, but was devoted to God. She began hearing voices that made her believe God had chosen her to give France victory over the English. Charles knew she was coming and, to test her, put another man on the throne, while he hid among the crowd. She had never seen the king before, yet she walked past everyone else in the crowded room and bowed before the real king. He still wasn't convinced, but then she told him what he had prayed for in his

Joan of Arc led the French to victory in the Hundred Years' War, but was burned at the stake as a heretic.

private chapel. Priests came to test her, but they left believing she was divinely inspired.

She was given command of the army, but the generals refused to obey her, until they discovered her voices won victories. Whenever they did not obey her, the French lost. Dressed in simple armor, she rode at the head of attacks, and common soldiers had such trust in her that they overcame stronger foes. The common English soldier lost courage and fought now with little enthusiasm. She drove the English from Rheims and witnessed proudly the crowning of her king.

Then her voices did not speak to her, and she wanted to return to Domrémy, but the king wanted her to attack English-held Paris. Joan was badly wounded in the battle, and French forces withdrew to Compiégne. The mayor raised the drawbridge as she approached the city, and she was captured by the Burgundians, allies of the English. They sold her to the English for the small sum of 16,000 francs. She was tried before English churchmen as a heretic who listened to voices. Her trial lasted a year, and during that time, Charles made no effort to ransom or rescue her.

Under the pressure of constant questioning, she was ready to recant (admit her sin), but the visions and voices returned and strengthened her resolve. She was found guilty of heresy and condemned to death.

At the marketplace of Rouen, she was burned at the stake in 1431. As the flames roared around her, she raised a rude cross made of firewood and, looking to heaven, said, "Jesus!" An English soldier, realizing the tragedy he had just witnessed, said: "We are lost. We have burnt a saint."

Despite all of the early successes at Crécy, Poitiers, and Agincourt, the English were never able to win any major battles again. Their army fought with little spirit or enthusiasm, while the French fought with revenge in their hearts. In 1453, the English sailed home defeated. The separate identities of France and England were now firmly established.

Name _____

Class _____

POINTS TO CONSIDER

1. What other examples might be given that show how the right person at the right time might turn a defeat into victory?

_____

_____

_____

_____

2. What questions would you ask of Charles if you were to interview him?

_____

_____

_____

_____

3. Why do you think the story of Joan of Arc has so fascinated people through the years?

_____

_____

_____

_____

Name _____

Class _____

CHALLENGES

1. Why had Charles VII never been crowned?

_____

_____

2. Where was Joan from, and what was her rank in society?

_____

_____

3. Why did she believe she had been chosen to drive the English out?

_____

_____

4. What made Charles believe she was telling the truth?

_____

5. Why did the French generals change their minds about her?

_____

6. What happened after she saw Charles crowned as king?

_____

7. Why did she attack Paris?

_____

8. What happened when she withdrew to Compiégne?

_____

_____

9. When she was tried for heresy, how much help did she receive from Charles?

_____

10. What happened after she was put to death?

_____

Doubts Flow
Like a River

In the Middle Ages, people accepted whatever they were told. They did not question the church, because it held the keys to heaven. They did not question their ruler, because he had a torture rack. They did not read the ancient writings, because few could read in any language. Their world was limited to a small village or town, and while they might have met a crusader or a sailor who had traveled hundreds of miles, there were oceans, continents, and peoples completely unknown to even him.

Thomas Aquinas said: "faith and reason are one," which left little room for honest doubt. But Peter Abelard said: "For by doubt, we come to investigate, and by investigation, we learn truth." By 1500, there were many doubts being expressed. Was the feudal system—with its lords, vassals, knights, and wars—the way society should be? Were some of the practices

Leonardo da Vinci was one of those people with a questioning mind that would lead the search for answers in the Renaissance.

within the church proper? Was alchemy good science? Should artists and writers be limited by the rigid standards of the past?

The church was soon to be challenged on many fronts. It had lost some of its influence during the time it was in France (the "Babylonian Captivity") and when two or three men at a time claimed to be Pope (the "Great Schism"). In the 12th century, St. Bernard criticized bishops and archbishops as tools of the devil, but Joachim of Floris went further and attacked the Pope as the Antichrist (enemy of Christ). Wycliffe and Huss blasted the evils in the church during their time, but failed to make much difference. Martin Luther and John Calvin in the early 16th century, however, succeeded in bringing dramatic change through the Protestant Reformation.

Traditional views on science were also being challenged by the 16th century. One major change was the growing doubt that the earth was the center of the universe. Aristarchus had written in the 3rd century that the sun was the center of the universe, but in the Middle Ages the theory of Ptolemy, going back to the 2nd century, that the earth was the center of the universe, was much more popular. Nicholas Copernicus was not the first to question Ptolemy's science, but through crude instruments and nights of study, he became convinced that the planets revolved around the sun. He knew this would be very unpopular, so he waited until he was on his deathbed before he published *On the Revolutions of the Heavenly Spheres* (1543). His views remained unpopular for many years, and when Galileo tried to defend them in the 17th century, he was imprisoned.

Galileo, Leonardo da Vinci, and others were beginning to develop a new understanding of physics. Knowledge of the human body was also increasing. In the 14th century, dissection of human bodies (cadavers) became a common practice at the University of Bologna. Andreas Vesalius became noted for his knowledge gained from dissections and is today known as the father of the science of anatomy. Michael Servetus studied the circulation of blood in the early 16th century.

Name _____

Class _____

POINTS TO CONSIDER

1. If the Minister for Science was a position open in the Middle Ages, who would be the most likely to cause scientific breakthroughs: Aquinas or Abelard? Why?

_____

_____

_____

_____

_____

2. Why was the question of whether the earth was the center of the universe so important to some people?

_____

_____

_____

_____

_____

3. Why was the use of human cadavers so important to knowledge about disease and the circulation of blood in the late Middle Ages?

_____

_____

_____

_____

_____

Name _____

Class _____

CHALLENGES

1. As a person who prefers to let others tell you what to believe, which would you like better: Aquinas or Abelard?

_____

2. As a person who enjoys thinking for yourself, which would you like better: Aquinas or Abelard?

_____

3. Whom did St. Bernard criticize?

_____

4. Who called the Pope the Antichrist?

_____

5. What movement did Luther and Calvin lead?

_____

6. Whose theory did people of the Middle Ages prefer: Aristarchus or Ptolemy? Why?

_____

_____

7. What theory did Copernicus develop?

_____

8. Whom did Galileo side with?

_____

9. What was an improvement made in medical studies at Bologna?

_____

_____

10. Who is known today as the father of medical anatomy?

_____

Powerful Kings Challenge Feudalism

Many things conspired to break feudalism, and one of the most important was the development of strong rulers and ruling families (dynasties). These took power away from the local lords who had controlled Europe's people for centuries. Events began to play into the hands of kings. The Black Death had wiped out many of the nobility. The church was less of a political force since it had been weakened by internal bickering. Growing cities were closely allied to their rulers; merchants needed trade, and it was far easier to move goods where there were fewer tax collectors. Cannons also made it easier for the king's army to keep local lords under control. In Portugal, Spain, England, and France, dynasties began to emerge.

Louis XI was one of the kings trying to take power from local lords and rule his kingdom with absolute authority.

John I led a successful revolt against the child ruler of Portugal and her Spanish regent in 1385. This established the Avis dynasty in Portugal, and after he defeated the Spanish at Aljubarrota, Portugal's independence was assured. John's son, Prince Henry, would play an important role in the age of discovery and is known as Henry the Navigator.

Louis XI got off to a poor start after becoming king of France in 1461, and his enemies formed the League of the Public Good against him. While they were united against him, he was powerless. Then he started dividing them against each other by creating suspicions and jealousies. He was known as the "universal spider" because of the webs he spun.

The marriage of Ferdinand of Aragon and Isabella of Castile in 1469 brought two powerful families together in Spain. They united the towns behind them, began breaking the resistance of feudal lords, restricted the power of the Pope over the Spanish church, and began seizing the property of Spanish Jews.

The English situation in 1455 was almost a classic Medieval situation. The weak, sometimes insane, King Henry VI (a Lancaster) was challenged by a rival family, the Yorks. The Lancaster's symbol (a red rose) and the York's symbol (a white rose) gave the War of the Roses its name. Edward IV (York) deposed Henry, but four years later, the Lancasters overthrew Edward and put Henry back on the throne. Then Edward came back and put Henry in the Tower of London. Edward's successor, Richard III, was overthrown by a Lancaster descendant, Henry Tudor, in 1485. Now called Henry VII, he married Edward IV's daughter and united the families, at least on paper.

After the Hundred Years' War and this civil war, the English people wanted order. Henry knew his rivals were being backed by foreign countries, so he worked to improve foreign relations by marrying off his sons and daughters to other rulers' children. His oldest son, Arthur, was an infant when Henry arranged for his marriage to Catherine of Aragon. His oldest daughter was married off to Scotland's king. Any English lord who dared oppose Henry faced his army and his Court of the Star Chamber, which had the power to arrest and torture anyone suspected of a crime.

Name _____

Class _____

POINTS TO CONSIDER

1. What methods were used by rulers to get and keep power that probably would not work today?

_____

_____

_____

_____

2. What ways were used by rulers that a dictator might use today?

_____

_____

_____

_____

3. Which of the rulers mentioned in this section do you think would make the best politician today? Why?

_____

_____

_____

_____

128

Name _____

Class _____

CHALLENGES

1. How was the Black Death helpful to kings?

_____

_____

2. How did cities feel about the growing power of kings? Why?

_____

_____

3. What was the name of the ruling family of Portugal?

_____

4. Who was King John of Portugal's most famous son?

_____

5. How did Louis XI weaken his enemies?

_____

_____

6. What nickname was given to Louis XI?

_____

7. How did the War of the Roses get its name?

_____

8. How did Henry Tudor win the support of the Yorks?

_____

9. How did Henry VII win support from Scotland?

_____

10. What court did Henry VII establish that scared anyone who opposed him?

Feudalism Falls
Victim to the Pen

It is said that the month of March roars in like a lion and leaves like a lamb. Perhaps the same could be said for feudalism. It began with barbarian invasions, when European civilization was threatened by Goths, Vandals, Lombards, Huns, and Normans. At the end, these barbarians were farmers, merchants, sailors, and priests, no different than those they had conquered.

No newspapers announced when the Middle Ages were over and the Renaissance began. But what were some signs that changes were taking place? Explorers like Columbus, who managed to find a New World, or Magellan, whose crew sailed around the planet? Or new, powerful kings who seized

Don Quixote, the fictional knight created by Cervantes, symbolized those still trying to hold on to the outdated way of life of the medieval period.

power from the feudal lords and built nations? Or artists like Michelangelo and Leonardo da Vinci, who made pictures on canvas seem lifelike, or who turned stone into angels? Or reformers like Wycliffe, Huss, Luther, and Calvin, who criticized the church and forced it to change its ways? All of these were part of the change, but for a person of the time, a better sign may have been the criticism of feudalism from clever writers who made people think about the events of the Middle Ages in a new and critical way.

Baldassare Castiglione wrote the *Book of the Courtier* (1515), which listed the requirements to be a true nobleman: he must be good at war, but it was as important to be tactful, modest, gracious, understand the importance of art and music, read widely, and express himself well in writing.

Francois Rabelais, a former priest turned doctor, preferred writing over either profession. His books, *Gargantua* and *Pantagruel* (1534) were criticisms of the educational system, the dull life of monks, and the strict rules by which people lived. In his opinion, enjoying life and doing as one pleased was far better. Much of his humor is not funny today, but must have been hilarious to the people of his time.

A French writer, Michel de Montaigne, wrote his *Essays* in 1580. Among other subjects, he criticized the religious wars that were destroying Europe. With the voice of wisdom he said it showed great self-love for a person to destroy public peace so they could have their way.

In England, William Shakespeare covered many Medieval themes in his plays: the feeble excuses for wars in *Henry V,* bloody feuds in *Romeo and Juliet,* the prejudice against Jews in *The Merchant of Venice,* and the tragic results of the greed for power in *Macbeth* and *Hamlet.*

But it was Miguel de Cervantes who may have put the last nail in feudalism's coffin with his knight, *Don Quixote,* who with his trusted squire, Sancho Panza, goes out to rid the world of evil. Unfortunately, Quixote cannot tell the difference between the real world and his imaginary world where chivalry and courtly love will save the day. Instead of making the world better, he often confuses it more than ever.

A new age had arrived—Renaissance—with its expanding knowledge of the world, cities, technology, education, and faith in the human ability to control history.

Name _____

Class _____

POINTS TO CONSIDER

1. What were major signs that the Medieval period was nearing its end? Do you think the average person understood the changes going on around them? Explain.

_____

_____

_____

_____

2. If you were a writer ridiculing the 20th century, what might be some topics that you would bring up?

_____

_____

_____

_____

3. Which would be more like the modern world: the Medieval or the Renaissance periods in history? Explain your answer.

_____

_____

_____

_____

Name _____

Class _____

CHALLENGES

1. Name two explorers who helped end the Middle Ages.

_____

2. Name two artists who brought about change.

_____

3. Name four church reformers who ended the hold of the Medieval church.

_____

4. Who thought the true nobleman must also be a gentleman?

_____

5. Who thought people should enjoy themselves and not worry about rules?

_____

6. What did Montaigne believe was the cause of the religious wars?

_____

_____

7. In what play did Shakespeare write about the bloody feuds that brought tragedy to Italian city states?

_____

8. What play by Shakespeare discusses the prejudice against Jews?

_____

9. What is Don Quixote's purpose in life?

_____

_____

10. What is the age following the Middle Ages called?

_____

ANSWERS TO CHALLENGES

The Roman Empire in its Glory (page 3)
1. Rivers: Rhine and Danube.
2. African valley: Nile.
3. The *Mare Nostrum*: Mediterranean.
4. Highways: Appian and Flaminian Ways
5. City: London.
6. Greek city: Athens.
7. Galleys: wind and slaves.
8. *"Pax Romana"* means Peace of Rome.
9. Citizen: No.
10. Language: Latin.

The Roman Empire in Decay (page 6)
1. Percentage: one in ten (10 percent).
2. Paul said he was born a Roman citizen.
3. Punishment: hanging from a cross.
4. Taxpayers did not want them there in the first place.
5. Unemployment high because poor people could not compete with slave labor.
6. Poor given bread and entertainment.
7. Races at Circus Maximus.
8. Gladiators at Colosseum.
9. Emperors: Nero, Caligula, and Diocletian.
10. Saw cross in sky: Constantine.

Reasons for the Fall of Rome (page 9)
1. Constantinople on west side of Bosporus.
2. Longest: Constantinople.
3. Ambitious could not move up in status.
4. Veto: tribunes.
5. Protector of morals: censor.
6. Protectors of emperor: Praetorian Guard.
7. Best soldiers: Germans.
8. Upper class: patricians. Lower class: plebeians.
9. Subject: history.
10. They could not work together against the barbarians.

A Mustard Seed that Threatened Imperial Power (page 12)
1. Biographies: Matthew, Mark, Luke, John.
2. Book: Acts of the Apostles.
3. Leaders: bishops.
4. Peter: Bishop of Rome.
5. Responsible for Peter's death: Nero.
6. Christians refused to make emperor a god and made poor soldiers.
7. Diocletian: Christians to accept him as a god or die.
8. Meeting: Council of Nicaea.
9. Name: Julian the Apostate.
10. Name given: Pope.

Barbarians at the Gate (page 15)
1. Constantinople: Ostrogoths. Rome: Visigoths.
2. Goths defeated by Huns.
3. Lost battle: Eastern Roman Empire.
4. Attacked West: Vandals and Burgundians.
5. Gaul: France.
6. Destroyers: Vandals.
7. Saved Rome: Bishop Leo.
8. Nation: Hungary.
9. Ended Roman Empire: Odoacer.
10. Last Roman emperor: Romulus Augustulus.

Barbarians Take Charge (page 18)
1. Artorius: King Arthur.
2. Saxon leader: Alfred the Great.
3. Norman leader: William the Conqueror.
4. Goth: Theodoric.
5. Frankish king: Merovich.
6. Clovis's conversion: He asked for God's help in fighting a battle; when he won, he converted.
7. Visigoths went to Spain and made Toledo capital.
8. Nations: France and Germany.
9. Clovis's reward: was made consul.
10. After death, land divided among his four sons.

Islam: a New Threat to Europe (page 21)
1. Occupations: camel driver and traveling merchant.
2. Convinced by Christians and Jews.
3. He angered supporters of the 300 gods at Mecca.
4. Year One begins with Hegira (flight) from Mecca.
5. Jihad: holy war.
6. Pillars: Straits of Gibralter.
7. Stopped advance: Charles Martel (The Hammer).
8. Moors withdrew to Spain and set up kingdoms.
9. Philosopher: Aristotle.
10. Learned cleanliness, arts of diagnosis, and uses of drugs.

Charlemagne Rises Above the Rest (page 24)
1. Ran kingdom: Mayor of the Palace.
2. Persuaded Pope: Pepin and Boniface.
3. Reason: Carloman retired to monastery.
4. Choice: convert or die.
5. Crowned Charles: Pope Leo III.
6. Name: Charlemagne (Charles the Great).
7. Officials in counties: count and bishop or archbishop.
8. Missi domenici: made sure local officials honest and not abusing people.
9. Wives 4; children 18.
10. Interests: science, law, literature, and religion.

Viking Plague from the North (page 27)
1. Ships decorated with head of snake or dragon.
2. Ancestors of Swedes, Norwegians, and Danes.
3. Decision by Folkmoot.
4. Fiercest warriors: Berserkers.
5. Main gods: Odin and Thor.
6. Targets: coastal towns, churches, and monasteries.
7. Explorer: Leif Ericson; Vinland.
8. Group: Normans.
9. Leader of attack: William the Conqueror.
10. System: feudalism.

Feudalism Comes to Europe (page 30)
1. Title: vassal.
2. One giving help: lord.
3. Vassal: servant for life.
4. Lord of nobles: king.
5. French king could not order noble's peasant around.
6. Land noble received: fief (or fiefdom).
7. If defensive war, served until war over.
8. Vassal punished by court made up of other vassals.
9. At most, could fight four days.
10. Seasons: winter and harvest.

Showdown at Canossa (page 33)
1. Ceremony: lay investiture.
2. Pope: by clergy around Rome.
3. Group: College of Cardinals.
4. Simony: buying and selling church offices.
5. Meeting: Cluny, France.
6. Pope: Gregory VII (Hildebrand).
7. Bishops: should be chosen by Pope.
8. Emperor: Henry IV.
9. Emperor stood barefoot in snow 3 days.
10. Antipope: one installed as rival to real Pope.

Great Minds in the Dark Ages (page 36)
1. Augustine: sold what he had and gave it to the poor.
2. War justified if it was last resort and fought for a just cause.
3. Scholar: Bede.
4. Profession: teacher.
5. *Sic et Non* gave both sides of issues.
6. Doubts bad: no.
7. Argument: ownership of church lands.
8. Becket killed by four barons.
9. Nature: Francis of Assisi.
10. Aquinas: because believed in democracy and public participation.

Monks and Hermits Reject the World (page 39)
1. Stylites lived on a 60-foot pillar for 30 years.
2. First monastery: St. Anthony.
3. Women's version: convents.
4. First rule: total obedience.
5. Work day: 6 a.m. to sunset.
6. Four orders: Franciscans, Dominicans, Carmelites, Augustinian Hermits.
7. Identifiable by their cloak.
8. Other name: nunnery.
9. Political because abbot was vassal.
10. Areas they improved: education, care for sick, safety for traveler.

Rulers with "Uneasy Heads" (page 42)
1. Hugh Capet elected by nobles of northern France.
2. Hugh had no national army or tax sources.
3. Pound: weight of 240 pennies.
4. 20 shillings in pound.
5. Matilda had better claim to throne than Stephen.
6. Nobles built forts in defiance of law.
7. Matilda overthrew Stephen and put him in prison.
8. Reason: Matilda too cruel.
9. Matilda put in prison and later escaped to France.
10. First Holy Roman Emperor: Otto I.

The Nobility of Europe (page 45)
1. First: duke.
2. First: viscount.
3. First: countess.
4. Replaced: viscount.
5. Title: baron.
6. Defense: boiling water, rocks, arrows.
7. Attack: catapults and battering rams.
8. Ordeal: to determine guilt or innocence.
9. Combat: fought each other.
10. Defenses of church, chivalry, crusades.

Knights in Shining Armor (page 48)
1. Used knights: Charles Martel.
2. Purpose: to fight wars.
3. Training: followed lord into battle, carried shield and spear.
4. Manners: politeness, courtesy, helpfulness.
5. Saints: Michael and George.
6. French: Knights Hospitalers.
7. International: Knights Templars.
8. Crossbow could penetrate armor.
9. Strategy: get him on ground; weight made him defenseless.
10. It declined because family connection more important than service.

Answers to Challenges (continued)

Ladies of the Court (page 51)
1. Aristotle said women inferior.
2. Paul said women should be silent in the church.
3. Germanic law treated women as husband's property.
4. He saw if she could benefit him financially or politically.
5. Not very: nobility often arranged marriage through letters and contracts.
6. Troubadours sang love songs to women.
7. Relationship between Lancelot and Guinevere.
8. Norman women wanted husbands to go home.
9. Effect: husbands went home.
10. Chaucer said to give him what he pleased.

The Byzantine Empire Is in Trouble (page 54)
1. Important because was at crossroads of east-west trade.
2. Code: Justinian.
3. Made law: emperor.
4. After death: struggle to replace him.
5. Invaders: Slavic, Bulgarians, Petchenegs, and Russians.
6. Title: patriarch.
7. Rules: bishops couldn't marry, but other priests could.
8. Break: 1054.
9. Asked: Emperor Alexius I.
10. Decided to help: Urban II.

"God wills it!" The First Crusade (page 57)
1. Speech at Clermont, France.
2. Promise: everlasting life in heaven.
3. Symbol: cross on tunics.
4. Stirred up support: Peter the Hermit.
5. Commoners: wiped out.
6. Motives: religion and greed.
7. Knight leaders: Robert, Godfrey, and Bohemund.
8. Lance that pierced Jesus's side.
9. After taking Jerusalem: killed 10,000 Jews and Moslems.
10. Jerusalem: Saladin

Richard the Lion Hearted and the Third Crusade (page 60)
1. Rulers: Richard, Philip II, and Frederick Barbarossa.
2. Legendary: Robin Hood.
3. Richard's parents: Henry II and Eleanor of Aquitaine.
4. At Acre: French.
5. Sultan: Saladin.
6. Tries: 4.
7. Captured at Vienna.
8. Ransom: Henry VI.
9. Demanded: 150,000 marks.
10. After return: went to France.

The Crusading Spirit Declines (page 63)
1. Attacked: Zara and Constantinople.
2. Pope threatened them with excommunication.
3. Children believed their innocence could do more than that of older crusaders.
4. Children died crossing Alps or in slavery.
5. Fifth Crusade: captured Damietta in Egypt.
6. After battle, forced to give Damietta back.
7. Seventh Crusade started by Louis IX.
8. Louis IX was captured and held for ransom.
9. Eighth Crusade tried to capture Tunis.
10. Louis died, and crusaders returned home.

A Legal System Develops in England (page 66)
1. Civil cases: property.
2. Criminal case: government.
3. Being sued: Black.
4. Punishments: fine, prison, or death.
5. Juror: to find evidence and bring it to attention of sheriff.
6. Charges: presentments.
7. Petit jury: to decide guilt or innocence.
8. Judges went to the "Year Book."
9. Moots: practice trials by law students.
10. Languages: English, Latin, and Norman French.

King John Signs the Magna Carta (page 69)
1. Son: John.
2. Preceded: Richard the Lion Hearted.
3. John threatened any noble who obeyed the Pope.
4. Leader: Stephen Langton.
5. John had raised taxes on the nobles.
6. Meaning: Great Charter.
7. John signed with seal (he couldn't write).
8. Officials must know the law and obey it.
9. Consent: no taxation without representation.
10. Judgment of peers: jury.

Castles and Forts Give More Power to the Nobility (page 72)
1. Castles main quality: safety.
2. Castle to keep out unwanted intruders, feel safe from other lords or commoners.
3. Tapestries hung for color and to cut down the draft.
4. Baileys: grassy areas between walls, place for livestock to graze during a siege.
5. Moat: ditch filled with water.
6. Ram: break through doors and gates of castle.
7. Battlements: to give better angle to shoot at enemy.
8. Keep: tall tower where baron lives.
9. In keep: baron's family and some guards.
10. Keep has wells and storage places.

Cities Grow in Size and Influence (page 75)
1. Name: Lutetia (Mudtown).
2. Romans built road network.
3. Name: Londonium.
4. Bourg: fort where people could go for safety.
5. River cities built drawbridges.
6. Wealthy: around center of city.
7. Center: market place, ruler's palace, and cathedral.
8. Poor lived at outer edge.
9. New walls built when city outgrew space in old walls.
10. Old walls: sometimes kept them, and others were torn down.

Cathedrals: Monuments to Faith (page 78)
1. Name: from the bishop's chair called a cathedra.
2. Style: Romanesque.
3. Wall supports: flying buttresses.
4. Doors like hands at prayer.
5. Glass makers: glaziers.
6. East-west: nave.
7. North-south: transepts.
8. Altar-choir area: apse.
9. To become a mason: 7 years.
10. Mason shortage: kept out competition, and many died from lung disease.

Medieval Universities: Centers of Learning (page 81)
1. Scholar came to town, and students came to learn from him.
2. Language: Latin.
3. Section: Latin Quarter.
4. Sorbon gave money for 16 poor students to have a hall in which to live.
5. Complaints: overcharged for food and lodging.
6. *Universitas*: All who belong to the guild.
7. Medical school: Salerno.
8. Law: Bologna.
9. Degree: B.A.
10. Careers: church, government, law, medicine.

Life in the Middle Ages: the Cities (page 84)
1. Live a year and a day.
2. Burgesses: because town built near fort (burgh).
3. Nouveaux riches: newly rich.
4. Guilds: workers or businessmen in same trade uniting.
5. Guilds blocked outside competition.
6. Venice: 22 guilds.
7. Italian navies: controlled trade on Mediterranean.
8. Men: to protect women from garbage dumped out of windows.
9. They moved the city.
10. Noted for crime: Rome.

Life in the Middle Ages: the Peasants' Lot (page 87)
1. Status: villein.
2. Serfs went with the land.
3. Crofters worked for nobles or rich villeins.
4. Groups for companionship and because oxen and plows too hard to work alone.
5. Peasant had to pay for entertainment and they tore up field he had worked.
6. French peasants: salt tax.
7. Revolt: Jacquerie Rebellion
8. Peasant had to pay head tax: everyone paid 1 shilling.
9. Hero: killed tax collector.
10. Targets: rich churchmen and nobles.

Life in the Middle Ages: Recreation (page 90)
1. Hawks trained to kill hares, pigeons, and herons.
2. Tournaments created to make practice for war more fun.
3. Winner got opponent's horse and arms.
4. Comedians: jesters.
5. Three occasions: feast days, planting, and harvest time.
6. Physical events: wrestling, jumping, bow and arrow competition, and tugs of war.
7. Plays got obscene.
8. Poacher's foot cut off.
9. Incense: soles of shoes burned.
10. Miracle plays: lives of saints.

Life in the Middle Ages: Literature (page 93)
1. Monsters: Grendel and his mother.
2. Fight: Saracens.
3. Roland blew his magic horn.
4. Nibelungs: Children of the mist.
5. Siegfried loves Kriemhild.
6. Brunhild: must defeat her in combat.
7. Travelers: Geoffrey Chaucer.
8. Story: *The Romance of the Rose.*
9. Guide: Beatrice.
10. Book: Gutenburg *Bible.*

Life in the Middle Ages: Art and Music (page 96)
1. Purchasers: churches, religious orders, and nobles.
2. Began by studying with a master.
3. Style spread through imitators.
4. Cimabue: unusual because was nobleman.
5. Boy: Giotto (many experts dispute the story).
6. Angelico trained as miniaturist.
7. Contribution: perspective, technique of having some figures appear closer than others.
8. General quality improving.
9. Music: Gregorian chant.
10. Songs: love ballads.

Life in the Middle Ages: Minorities (page 99)
1. Jews: artisans and tradesmen.
2. Jews became bankers because Christians not allowed to lend at interest.
3. Charged high interest because took great risk.
4. Expelled in 1290s.
5. Yiddish: a combination of German and Hebrew words written in Hebrew script.
6. Jews moved to Germany, Poland, and Russia.
7. Halevi wanted Jews to return to Jerusalem.
8. Spanish Jews treated well by Moslems.
9. Waldensians opposed having any clergy (priests).
10. Albigensians did not believe in fighting.

Life in the Middle Ages: Women (page 102)
1. Convenience: because of land or property she might have.
2. Interest: she didn't have any money.
3. Boy and girl in cradle could not be married.
4. Beating should be reasonable.
5. Cities: Paris and London.
6. Heloise: Peter Abelard.
7. Paris: refused to admit any more women students.
8. Professor: Maria di Novella.
9. Clare from wealthy noble family.
10. Poor Clares had to live in absolute poverty.

Life in the Middle Ages: Science (page 105)
1. Scientific method: observations, experiments, and logical conclusions.
2. Medicine: Galen.
3. Earth: Ptolemy.
4. Geber: sulfur and mercury.
5. Perfect metal: gold.
6. Gain from alchemy: learned about chemicals.
7. Bacon: eyeglasses.
8. Medicine: Paracelsus.
9. Disease: Avicenna
10. Alhazan: see images reflected from objects into our eyes.

Life in the Middle Ages: Health (page 108)
1. Baths: once or twice a year.
2. Life span: 30 to 40 years.
3. Swiss homes: didn't need hat or coat indoors.
4. People slept on straw on floor.
5. City odors: open sewers, manure, and garbage.
6. Stomach: dust from St. Martin's tomb.
7. Four humors: blood, phlegm, yellow bile, black bile.
8. Humors had to be in balance for person to be healthy.
9. Baldness: eat onions.
10. Monks: spiritual help (confession and communion).

The Black Death (page 111)
1. John: high fever and swollen lymph glands in neck.
2. Jeanne: hemorrhaging and vomiting blood.
3. Plague: 1347.
4. Cities hard hit because people were so overcrowded and contact greater.
5. Flagellation: to satisfy God's anger.
6. End: Pope Clement VI threatened to excommunicate them, and rulers forbade them from performing in their city.
7. Jews did not drink from wells.
8. Officers were afraid they might catch plague.
9. Percent: 25-33 percent.
10. Effect: ended feudal obligations, peasants started moving to cities, many priests died.

The Beginnings of Parliament (page 114)
1. Absolutism: unrestricted power.
2. Meetings: discuss major problems or get permission to raise taxes.
3. Witan: leaders of church and nobility.
4. King's Court: the Great Council was too large to be helpful.
5. Chancellor: king's most important advisor.
6. Checkered cloth: Chancellor of Exchequer.
7. Mad Parliament: king had let Pope and Frenchmen have too much influence.
8. Henry III then a rubber stamp approving Simon's policies.
9. Edward I: England at war with France and had Scottish and Welsh rebellions.
10. Houses: Lords and Commons.

The Church and its Critics (page 117)
1. *Clericos Laicos:* church property couldn't be taxed without Pope's permission.
2. Kings: began taking protection away from church.
3. *Unam Sanctum:* Pope could remove kings, and obeying the Pope was necessary for salvation.
4. Clement V went to Avignon.
5. Period: 1309-77; Babylonian Captivity.
6. Number: 3.
7. Confusion ended 1417.
8. Wycliffe: Popes and kings didn't care about the suffering of people.
9. Followers: wrote first English Bible.
10. Huss was burned at the stake.

The Hundred Years' War (page 120)
1. French helped Scots and people of Aquitaine oppose the English.
2. English had French allies who opposed the French king.
3. Edward III said the French throne was rightfully his.
4. Weapon: cannon.
5. Genoese had wet bows.
6. John wanted to stop raids by the Black Prince and wanted revenge for Crécy.
7. After battle, John captured and held for ransom.
8. English pride rose, and people pulled together.
9. Wat Tyler: head tax imposed on everyone over 15.
10. At Agincourt: heavy rainstorm made it difficult for French cavalry to attack.

Joan of Arc Steps In to Save the French (page 123)
1. Charles VII could not go to Rheims for his coronation; it was in English hands.
2. Joan from Domrémy; she was a peasant.
3. Believed because heard voices and saw visions.
4. Charles believed because she told him what he had prayed for in his chapel.
5. Generals: she always won, and when they ignored her, they lost.
6. After crowning: voices went away, and she wanted to go home.
7. Paris: king asked her to.
8. Approaching Compiégne: mayor pulled up draw bridge and she was captured.
9. Help: none.
10. After Joan's death: English lost battles and returned home defeated.

Doubts Flow Like a River (page 126)
1. Prefer: Aquinas.
2. Prefer: Abelard.
3. St. Bernard: bishops and archbishops.
4. Antichrist: Joachim of Floris.
5. Led: Protestant Reformation.
6. Ptolemy because he put earth at center which made them feel more important.
7. Copernicus: planets revolve around sun.
8. Galileo: with Copernicus.
9. Bologna: began dissecting human bodies.
10. Father of medical anatomy: Andreas Vesalius.

Powerful Kings Challenge Feudalism (page 129)
1. Black Death wiped out many noble families.
2. Cities liked powerful kings; few tax collectors bothered them.
3. Portugal: Avis.
4. Son: Henry the Navigator.
5. Louis XI: created suspicions and jealousies among them.
6. Nickname: "Universal spider."
7. Name: symbols of both families were roses (red for Lancasters, white for Yorks).
8. Henry Tudor: Married daughter of Edward IV.
9. Henry VII: Married daughter off to king of Scotland.
10. Court: Court of the Star Chamber.

Feudalism Falls Victim to the Pen (page 132)
1. Explorers: Columbus and Magellan.
2. Artists: Michelangelo and Leonardo da Vinci.
3. Reformers: Wycliffe, Huss, Luther, and Calvin.
4. Nobleman: Baldassare Castiglione.
5. Don't worry: Francois Rabelais.
6. Montaigne: great self-love.
7. Feuds: *Romeo and Juliet.*
8. Prejudice: *Merchant of Venice.*
9. Quixote: rid the world of evil.
10. Age: Renaissance.

Answers to *Noble Rankings: A Graphic Organizer (page 146)*

King/Queen
Prince/Princess
Duke/Duchess
Marquis/Marquise
Earl/Lady   Count/Countess
Viscount/Viscountess
Baron/Baroness
Baronet

Answer to *Identifying the Parts of a Castle (page 147)*

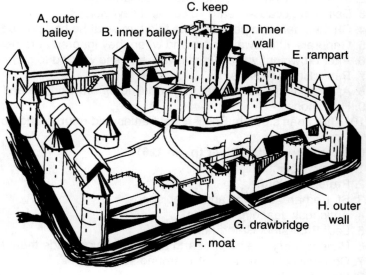

A. outer bailey
B. inner bailey
C. keep
D. inner wall
E. rampart
F. moat
G. drawbridge
H. outer wall

Answer to *Identifying the Parts of a Cathedral (page 148)*

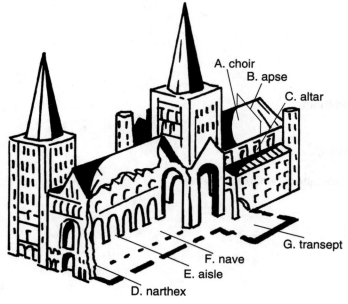

A. choir
B. apse
C. altar
D. narthex
E. aisle
F. nave
G. transept

Answers to *Matching Medieval Literature, Art, and Music (page 149)*

1. I, 2. F, 3. G, 4. L, 5. M,
6. J, 7. K, 8. C/E, 9. A,
10. C/E, 11. H, 12. N,
13. D, 14. B

Answers to *Bragging Contests*

Convention Room A (page 150) 1. Paul of Tarsus, 2. Nero, 3. Constantine, 4. Praetorian guard, 5. Julian, 6. Attila, 7. Romulus Augustulus, 8. Theodoric, 9. Clovis, 10. Mohammed, 11. Charles Martel, 12. Pepin,13. Missi Domenici, 14. a Viking, 15. Leif Ericson.

Convention Room B (page 151) 1. a vassal, 2. Gregory VII, 3. Henry IV, 4. Augustine, 5. Becket, 6. a hermit, 7. a nun, 8. Hugh Capet, 9. a marquis, 10. a knight, 11. a troubadour, 12. Guinevere, 13. Justinian,14. Urban II, 15. Robin Hood.

Convention Room C (page 152) 1. Louis IX, 2. Henry II, 3. King John, 4. Wat Tyler, 5. Chaucer, 6. Beowulf, 7. Cimabue, 8. Waldo, 9. a Jew, 10. Heloise, 11. an alchemist, 12. Henry III, 13. Huss, 14. John the Good, 15. Joan of Arc, 16. Copernicus, 17. Shakespeare.

Medieval Activites

Name Tags

Give each student a name tag with the name of someone from the Middle Ages and "Ask me about myself" written on it. Students should wear it throughout the Medieval part of the course. They should research their characters and be ready to answer questions about that person. By the end of the unit, they will know more about many people of the Middle Ages.

Possible characters include:

Abelard, an Albigensian, an alchemist, Angelico, Attila, Augustine, Roger Bacon, Thomas à Becket, a Black Death victim, Charlemagne, Charles VII (France), Charles Martel, Chaucer, Clovis, Copernicus, a crusader, Dante, Eleanor of Aquitaine, Francis of Assisi, a Goth, Gregory VII, Henry IV (Holy Roman Emperor), Henry VII (England), John Huss, a Jacquerie, a Medieval Jew, Joan of Arc, King John, Justinian (Byzantine), a knight, Leif Ericson, Mohammed, a monk, a nobleman, King Richard I (England), Simon de Montfort, King Stephen (England), a Medieval university student, a Viking, Wat Tyler, William the Conqueror, a noble woman, a peasant woman, John Wycliffe.

Heraldry

In the Middle Ages, noble families developed symbols called coats of arms, so that when they wore armor, people would be able to recognize them. The development of these symbols was called "heraldry," and it followed strict rules. All of the major encyclopedias have good discussions of heraldry for students to investigate. Have students develop a coat of arms for themselves or for their school or city. Then have them explain the reasons for the things they have put on the coat of arms.

To demonstrate that symbolism is still used today, you can also have students study national and state flags. They often have seals or symbols on them that the nation considers important. Have students develop a flag that represents their city or school and explain their reasons for the colors and symbols they chose for their flag.

Have students study the colors used for football, professional basketball, or hockey teams, and look for symbols that might be used on the uniforms or helmets. Ask students to explain what these colors and symbols say about a team.

Noble Rankings: A Graphic Organizer

Place each title pair (male and female) from the word bank in the correct box in the graphic organizer. Titles are ranked from the highest at the top to the lowest at the bottom.

Count/Countess	Prince/Princess	Baronet
King/Queen	Viscount/Viscountess	Duke/Duchess
Earl/Lady	Baron/Baroness	Marquis/Marquise

Name_____ Class_____

Identifying the Parts of a Castle

Label the castle parts using the choices in the word bank below. Place the correct choice on the line next to the corresponding part.

rampart
inner wall

keep
inner bailey

outer wall
drawbridge

moat
outer bailey

E.

D.

C.

B.

A.

H.

G.

F.

147

Identifying the Parts of a Cathedral

Label the cathedral parts using the choices in the word bank below. Place the correct choice on the line next to the corresponding part.

narthex	transept	choir	altar
nave	apse	aisle	

A._____

B._____

C._____

G._____

F._____

E._____

D._____

North

East

West

South

148

Matching Medieval Literature, Art, and Music

Match the literary, artistic, or musical work in column A with its creator or origin in column B. Place the correct letter from column B on the line next to the corresponding item in column A.

Column A

_____ 1. German love ballads

_____ 2. First Bible printed on a printing press

_____ 3. Paintings with perspective

_____ 4. *The Song of Roland*

_____ 5. *The Divine Comedy*

_____ 6. Gregorian Chant

_____ 7. Tales of King Arthur

_____ 8. *The Sagas of the Icelanders*

_____ 9. *Canterbury Tales*

_____ 10. *Beowulf*

_____ 11. Painting of St. Francis of Assisi

_____ 12. *The Nibelungs*

_____ 13. Realistic painting of the Madonna

_____ 14. Love ballads

Column B

A. Geoffrey Chaucer

B. troubadours

C. Norse legend

D. Cimabue

E. Norse legend

F. Gutenburg

G. Fra Angelico

H. Giotto

I. minnesingers

J. church music

K. Celtic legend

L. French legend

M. Dante

N. German legend

The Bragging Contest

At a convention of famous people from the Middle Ages, who could make the following statement about themselves? Place the correct name on the line by the corresponding statement.

Convention Room A

_____ 1. My guards were going to beat me until they found out I was a Roman citizen.

_____ 2. I was a Roman emperor who enjoyed persecuting Christians.

_____ 3. I saw a cross in the sky and became Christian.

_____ 4. My job was to protect the Roman emperor.

_____ 5. Christians called me "the Apostate."

_____ 6. Everyone feared me, except Bishop Leo.

_____ 7. I was the last emperor of Rome.

_____ 8. My people complained I was more Roman than Ostrogoth.

_____ 9. I was pagan until my wife's God helped me win a battle, and then I

converted.

_____ 10. My teachings are written in the Koran.

_____ 11. I drove the Moslems back at Tours and saved Europe for the Christians.

_____ 12. My son was the famous Charlemagne.

_____ 13. Charlemagne sent us out to catch dishonest officials.

_____ 14. Odin was my god before I converted.

_____ 15. I named my discovery "Vinland."

POSSIBLE ANSWERS

Attila	Clovis	Constantine	Julian
Charles Martel	Leif Ericson	Missi Domenici	Mohammed
Nero	Paul of Tarsus	Pepin	a Praetorian guard
Romulus Augustulus		Theodoric	a Viking

The Bragging Contest

At a convention of famous people from the Middle Ages, who could make the following statement about themselves? Place the correct name on the line by the corresponding statement.

Convention Room B

_____ 1. I gave up freedom for the protection of a powerful lord.

_____ 2. I was known as Hildebrand until I became Pope.

_____ 3. The Pope made me look stupid at Canossa, but I got even.

_____ 4. My most famous book is *The City of God.*

_____ 5. I was killed at Canterbury Cathedral.

_____ 6. People like me lived in deserts or on mountains.

_____ 7. I was a female Benedictine.

_____ 8. The nobles of northern France did not treat me like I was their king.

_____ 9. Originally, my title meant I was supposed to defend the frontier from the

barbarians.

_____ 10. I had to learn to fight, but I also had to learn how to be polite.

_____ 11. Ladies loved to hear me sing love ballads.

_____ 12. My husband was the famous King Arthur.

_____ 13. I wrote the legal code for the Byzantine Empire.

_____ 14. I was the Pope that started the First Crusade.

_____ 15. In legend, I saved England for King Richard while he was away on the

Third Crusade.

POSSIBLE ANSWERS

Augustine	Becket	Gregory VII	Guinevere
Henry IV	a hermit	Hugh Capet	Justinian
a knight	a marquis	a nun	Robin Hood
a troubadour	Urban II	a vassal	

The Bragging Contest

At a convention of famous people from the Middle Ages, who could make the following statement about themselves? Place the correct name on the line by the corresponding statement.

Convention Room C

_____ 1. I was taken prisoner on the Seventh Crusade.

_____ 2. I started the jury system in England.

_____ 3. I was forced to sign the Magna Carta.

_____ 4. An English peasant revolt was named for me.

_____ 5. I wrote about travelers on their way to London.

_____ 6. I killed Grendel and fought his mother.

_____ 7. My fame as an artist was surpassed by the artist I discovered.

_____ 8. I believed Christians should give their money to the poor.

_____ 9. I was forced to wear a yellow label and live in a ghetto.

_____ 10. My love for Abelard caused trouble for us.

_____ 11. I searched for the philosopher's stone.

_____ 12. I was sorry I called the "Mad Parliament."

_____ 13. The Council of Constance had me burned.

_____ 14. My desire for revenge at Poitiers backfired.

_____ 15. Charles VII did nothing to help me.

_____ 16. I believed earth was not the center of the universe.

_____ 17. I wrote *Romeo and Juliet* and *Hamlet*.

POSSIBLE ANSWERS

an alchemist	Beowulf	Chaucer	Cimabue
Copernicus	Heloise	Henry II	Henry III
Huss	a Jew	Joan of Arc	King John
John the Good	Louis IX	Shakespeare	Wat Tyler
Waldo			

BIBLIOGRAPHY

A person wishing to do further reading on any topic has to start somewhere. One suggestion is to read about the subject in a good encyclopedia. At the end of the article, there will be suggestions for further reading. Go to one of those sources on the list, and you will discover at the back of the book the bibliography that the author has used. Footnotes at the bottom of the page or the end of the chapter also give clues about where to find more information on that specific subject.

There are many books that cover the Middle Ages, but listed below are some that may prove useful to the teacher or student.

General references

Cambridge Medieval History, 8 vols. Cambridge: Cambridge University, 1911-36.

Cantor, Norman. *Medieval History.* New York: Macmillan, 1969.

Evans, Joan. *The Flowering of the Middle Ages.* London: Thames & Hudson, 1966.

Geanakoplos, Deno. *Medieval Western Civilization.* Lexington, Massachusetts, 1979.

Heer, Friedrich. *The Medieval World: Europe: 1100-1350.* Cleveland: World, 1961.

Peters, Edward. *Europe and the Middle Ages.* Englewood Cliffs, New Jersey: Prentice-Hall, 1983.

Previté-Orton, C.W. *The Shorter Cambridge Medieval History,* 2 volumes. Cambridge: Cambridge University, 1978.

Rice, David (ed.). *The Dark Ages.* London: Thames & Hudson, 1965.

Stephenson, Carl. *Medieval History: Europe from the Second to the Sixteenth Century.* New York: Harper, 1951.

Specific references

Allen, James. *Castles and Mansions.* Minneapolis: Lerner, 1989.

Baron, Salo. *A Social and Religious History of the Jews.* New York: Columbia University, 1957.

Barraclough, Geoffrey. *The Origins of Modern Germany.* New York: Oxford University, 1963.

Billings, Malcom. *The Cross and Crescent.* New York: Sterling, 1990.

Bloch, Marc. *Feudal Society.* Chicago: University of Chicago, 1961.

Cascardi, Anthony. *The Bounds of Reason: Cervantes.* Denver: Colorado University, 1986.

Clark, George (ed.). *The Oxford History of England,* 6 vols. Oxford: Oxford University, 1937-62.

Costain, Thomas. *The Magnificent Century.* New York: Popular Library, 1961.

Cross, F.L. (ed.). *The Oxford Dictionary of the Christian Church.* Oxford: Oxford University, 1972.

Coulton, G.G. *Medieval Panorama: The English Scene.* New York: Norton, 1974.

The Divine Campaigns [Crusades]. Alexandria, Virginia: Time-Life, 1989.

Donner, Fred. *Early Islamic Conquests.* Princeton: Princeton University, 1981.

Duby, Georges. *The Chivalrous Society.* Berkeley: University of California, 1977.

Elton, G.R. *England under the Tudors.* New York: Routledge, 1991.

Faber, G.S. *The History of Albigenses.* Gatlin, Tennessee: Church History, 1990.

Fawtier, Robert. *The Capetian Kings of France.* New York: Barnes & Noble, 1962.

Gabrieli, Francesco. *Muhammad and the Conquests of Islam.* New York: McGraw-Hill, 1968.

Gairdner, James. *Henry VII.* New York: Macmillan, 1892.

Gordon, C. *The Age of Attila.* Orlando: Marboro, 1992.

Guy, John. *Tudor England.* Oxford: Oxford University, 1988.

Kendall, Paul. *Louis XI: The Universal Spider.* New York: Norton, 1986.

Kenny, Anthony. *Wyclif in His Time.* Oxford: Oxford University, 1986.

McMahon, Clara. *Education in 15th Century England.* Westport, Connecticut: Greenwood, 1969.

Myers, A.R. *England in the Late Middle Ages.* New York: Pelican, 1978.

O'Callaghan, J.F. *A History of Medieval Spain.* Ithaca, New York: Cornell University, 1975.

Oman, Charles. *Great Revolt of 1381* [Wat Tyler]. Westport, Connecticut: Greenwood, 1969.

Powell, Neil. *Alchemy, the Ancient Science.* London: Danbury, 1976.

Richardson, H.G. and G.O. Sayles. *The English Parliament in the Middle Ages.* Rio Grande, Ohio: Hambledon, 1981.

Roskell, J.S. *Parliament and Politics in Late Medieval England.* Rio Grande, Ohio: Hambledon, 1985.

Runciman, Steven. *History of the Crusades.* Cambridge: Cambridge University, 1987.

Southern, R.W. *Western Society and the Church in the Middle Ages.* Baltimore: Penguin, 1970.

Stuard, Susan. *Women in Medieval Society.* Philadelphia: University of Pennsylvania, 1976.

Tuchman, Barbara. *A Distant Mirror: the Calamatous 14th Century.* New York: Knopf, 1978.

Vail, M.G. *Charles VII.* San Francisco: University of California, 1974.

Walsh, James. *13th, Greatest of Centuries.* New York: Fordham, 1907.